Perfectly Normal

Perfectly Normal

A Woman's Guide to Living with Low Libido

Dr Sandra Pertot

RODALE

This edition first published in the UK in 2005 by
Rodale International Ltd
7–10 Chandos Street
London W1G 9AD
www.rodale.co.uk

Printed and bound in the UK by CPI Bath using acid-free paper from sustainable sources.

Book design by Christina Gaugler

1 3 5 7 9 8 6 4 2

A CIP record for this book is available from the British Library

ISBN 1-4050-7759-X

This paperback edition distributed to the book trade by Pan Macmillan

Notice
This book is intended as a reference volume only, not as a medical manual. The information given here is designed to help you make informed decisions about your health. It is not intended as a substitute for any treatment that you may have been prescribed by your doctor. If you suspect that you have a medical problem, we urge you to seek competent medical help.

Mention of specific companies, organizations or authorities in this book does not imply endorsement by the publisher, nor does mention of specific companies, organizations or authorities in the book imply that they endorse the book.

Addresses, websites and telephone numbers given in this book were accurate at the time the book went to press.

RODALE
LIVE YOUR WHOLE LIFE™

We inspire and enable people to improve their lives and the world around them

In memory of my father,
Raymond George Wortley
(born Frederick James),
a good dad.

Contents

Acknowledgments

THERE ARE ALWAYS MANY PEOPLE who play vital roles in the writing and publication of a book.

I am grateful to my agent, Robbie Anna Hare, for her encouragement and wise counsel when this book was in its early stages and throughout the entire process. My thanks also go to Margot Schupf, executive editor of Lifestyle Books at Rodale, who saw through the stereotypes and took a chance on a book out of left field. Thanks also to Christine Bucks, my editor at Rodale, who has been a patient and meticulous collaborator.

I have been extremely lucky to spend more than 30 years in a profession that has always been intriguing and satisfying. A large part of my enjoyment of my profession has been the privilege of sharing the lives of so many good people. Without their trust, this book could never have been written.

Several relatives, friends, and colleagues read an early draft of my work, and their comments were invaluable; thanks to you all.

And finally, my deepest thanks go to my husband, Rudi; my children, Jane and Simon; my parents, Ray and Cath Wortley; and the many members of my extended family, who over a lifetime have provided me with the love, joy, and security that is the bedrock of it all.

INTRODUCTION

Commonsense Solutions to an Everyday Sexual Problem

FOR SOMETHING THAT IS SUPPOSED to be the source of so much pleasure, sex seems to cause an awful lot of pain for many people. For over 30 years, I have listened to men and women pour out their worries about their sex lives, and I sometimes think that there have been enough tears shed in my office to fill a small lake.

The problems that people bring to a sex therapist are varied. Women worry about why they take so long to become aroused, men are concerned that they can't last long enough, parents ask whether it's normal for their young child to explore his genitals, a woman is upset that her partner reads girly magazines or calls a phone sex service, a caregiver needs some advice about an elderly man who has started to act inappropriately—and these are the more routine cases.

For all this variety, by far the largest number of people seeking sex therapy are women who rarely feel any need or desire for sex.

Often, women begin to outline their problem by stating, "There must be something wrong with me—I never feel like sex." It's the phrase "something wrong with me" that has caught my attention over the years. As the women cry in their distress, they reveal their fears that they must be deeply flawed in some way for not having the hot and urgent sex drive that they believe everybody is supposed to have.

Early in my career, I began to realize that most of the women who came to see me were normal people who were living ordinary lives and that it seemed wrong to look for signs of pathology hidden deep in their psyches. I also found the alternative belief—that if a woman doesn't have a psychological problem to account for her low libido, there must be serious unresolved issues in her relationship with her partner—destructive rather than helpful in many cases.

So I turned the problem around and asked the question, "If a woman is perfectly normal, what might reasonably account for her low libido?"—and the surprising thing was that often, her lack of interest in sex made sense. Perhaps she was someone with a naturally low libido; perhaps the right things weren't being done to get her interested; perhaps what she was expecting sex drive to feel like was unrealistic; perhaps there were life stresses that were depressing her sex drive; perhaps her partner didn't understand her particular sexual needs. There are many ordinary and logical reasons that may account for a woman not experiencing a strong urge to have sex.

I discovered that the majority of women and their partners don't need prolonged sex therapy; they just need help making sense of what is happening. This makes it possible for them to trust themselves to develop the sex life that works for them, even if it is different from the stereotypes of great sex that dominate the media.

The problem is that there is so much hype about sex in our society that it's difficult for a woman to get straightforward, down-to-earth information about female sexuality. I began writing about sexual issues in the early 1980s, focusing on commonsense solutions to everyday sexual problems, and eventually the idea for this book was born. Although some sexual problems are complicated by serious issues and require intensive sex therapy, it's more likely than not that you are being conned into believing that you have a serious sexual problem when in fact you are perfectly normal. I hope this book sheds some light on your particular sexual worries so your tears will stop flowing.

PART I

The Sexual Illusion

CHAPTER 1

THE CHANGING VIEW OF NORMAL FEMALE SEXUALITY

"I never feel like [having] sex," says Julia. "What's wrong with me?
When I know Tom wants sex, I usually feel that I just can't be
bothered. He's upset because I always seem to be saying no,
and I never come on to him."

THERE IS NOTHING OBVIOUS TO DISTINGUISH JULIA FROM OTHER WOMEN. She could be a businesswoman or a housewife, twenty-something or in her midlife, in a caring relationship or one that is emotionally barren. She is just as likely to be fit and healthy as she is to be overweight and run-down. She may once have felt very strong sexual desire or have always had little energy for sex. There are many women who feel like Julia does, and they may have only one thing in common: They sometimes think that they wouldn't care if they never had sex again.

IN TODAY'S WORLD, young women expect to want sex with passion and enjoy it with abandon. A good sex life is regarded as a right that is taken for granted. With increasing recognition of women's rights in both the personal and public domains, women are no longer expected to play a subservient role to men in their personal relationships, and positive images of female sexuality are the norm. Lead characters in books and movies are routinely portrayed as sexually confident women, and numerous books and magazine articles are dedicated to helping the average real-life woman discover her sexual potential.

Of course, female sexuality hasn't always been viewed so positively. During the past century, female sexuality was variously denied, trivialized, repressed, and subjugated. To understand our current view of female sexuality, we have to start by looking to the past.

FEMALE SEXUALITY IN THE 20TH CENTURY

Medical and religious writers in the early decades of the 20th century viewed sex as a necessary evil that should be controlled at all times. They thought that masturbation, for example, could lead to mental or physical illness and even early death. Men were unfortunately more susceptible to the evils of sex, but women, mercifully, were often spared. Influential writers such as Dr. William Acton believed that normal women lacked sexual feelings of any kind and had sex only to please their husbands or to become pregnant.

Not everyone shared this view. The famous Viennese psychiatrist Dr. Sigmund Freud believed that sexual pleasure was a basic need for both men and women. However, he wasn't at all confident that women could mature enough to reach their sexual potential. Writing in the early part of the century, Dr. Freud had a powerful negative influence on the understanding of the sexual nature of women. He characterized them as mutilated males, biologically inferior because they lacked penises. And he insisted that an essential phase in the psychosexual development of women was acquiring the ability to achieve orgasm from penile thrusting alone. Although he recognized that the clitoris was highly sensitive and the vagina relatively insensitive, he stated that the inability of a woman to achieve orgasm with only the stimulation of intercourse was an indication of severe personality disorder.

The legacy of writers such as Acton and Freud continued into the second half of the century. In 1972, British sex educator Clare Raynor echoed Acton by declaring that though men have strong sex drives, women want sex only for babymaking. Many experts continued to support Freud's view that it might be difficult for women to mature sufficiently enough to come to orgasm during intercourse, and writers such as Canadian gynecologist Dr. Marion Hilliard, advised women not to be selfish and to consider their partner's feelings. This meant that sometimes they should fake arousal and orgasm so that their partner could feel proud and confident as a man.

Maxine Davis, a popular author in the 1950s whose books were still highly regarded and read decades later, gave women some conflicting advice. She advised young wives that it was their responsibility to adapt themselves to their husband's needs in order to have a successful marriage, because their own sexual pleasure wasn't an essential part of lovemaking. Like Raynor, she advised women to sometimes fake orgasm, but she also recommended that they come to climax during intercourse at least some of the time, because this was the only true path to sexual ecstasy. At the same time, Davis felt that they should never take charge, because she believed that men don't like bossy women.

In the early 1960s, popular psychologist Joyce Brothers, Ph.D., advised women who did indeed desire sex to not make it too obvious. She felt that for a marriage to be good, the husband had to dominate both sexually and financially. Wives could certainly work outside the home, provided they didn't have a more-responsible and more-financially successful job than their husband did, and they could want and even enjoy sex as long as they weren't too aggressive about it and allowed their husband to set the sexual pace.

It's no wonder that many women found the whole notion of sex confusing. Premaritally, it was the woman's responsibility to control any sexual behavior to avoid pregnancy, and within marriage, she should not be too keen on having sex but certainly be prepared to do her conjugal duty. If she was doing her marital duty, maybe she could or should enjoy it and perhaps even have an orgasm but only if she could do it in the normal way (that is, through intercourse). Even then, because of the absence of realistic sex education, there was a good chance that a woman wouldn't know what intercourse actually was—the wedding night was something of a shock to many a virgin bride. And if she did know what was expected of her, how did she know? Was she "that kind of girl"?

While there were some writers who questioned the notion that sex was inherently sinful and tried to bring some enlightenment into the lives of married couples, overall, society remained essentially conservative. Married couples had limited access to information on sexual matters, and girls were typically denied even basic information about menstruation, so the onset of menarche was often terrifying.

All that was about to change.

The Cultural Shift

When world-renowned sex researchers Dr. William Masters and Virginia Johnson published their groundbreaking work *Human Sexual Inadequacy* in 1970, they estimated that as many as 50 percent of couples led unsatisfying sex lives. At that time, they believed that the most significant causes of sexual problems were conservative cultural attitudes about sex, and ignorance about basic sexual functioning.

As difficult as it may be to believe now, the extent of sexual ignorance at that time was such that most people were unaware of the existence of the clitoris; many young brides had no idea that men had erections; and even into the 1970s, there were some couples whose apparent infertility was due to the fact the wife was still a virgin—neither partner knew where to put the penis!

It was assumed that a man knew more about sex and had to be patient with his virgin partner, guiding her through the mysteries of sex. It isn't clear how men were supposed to acquire this greater sexual knowledge and understanding, because sex education seems to have consisted of furtive schoolyard discussions, awkward "talks" from parents, and what was learned by self-discovery. If sex education in any formal sense did occur, it concentrated on reproduction and the immorality of premarital sex and masturbation; techniques for sexual pleasure were certainly not on the agenda.

There were many influences that combined in the 1960s to help shape a significant shift in our attitudes toward sex over the subsequent decades. These changes provided a climate for Masters and Johnson's work that had not existed before (although their ideas still met with considerable hostility from the conservative sections of society).

One of the most significant of these changes was the development of the contraceptive pill. Effective contraception meant that couples could explore sex for pleasure without fear of unwanted pregnancy. Still, no one, not even the sex researchers, asked the obvious question: *What makes sex pleasurable?* Instead, it was assumed that sexual pleasure was inevitable with certain sexual behaviors and that appropriate sex education would give couples all the information they needed.

Improved contraception led to a new phase in the women's movement. Control of fertility meant the opportunity to explore other life choices and redefine relationships with men. Women began to question the traditional view of sex as a wifely duty. The view of women as sexually naive and disinterested was seriously challenged during the 1960s, and for many women, being expected to endure male caresses without consideration for their own enjoyment was no longer acceptable. More and more women wanted a part of the "sex for pleasure" movement, and they developed the confidence to seek it. Not only that, many women felt strongly that they should participate in sex only when they felt like it. Saying no to your partner was becoming accepted as a fundamental right.

This change in focus away from reproduction and marital duty drew attention to the problems of people who did not automatically find sex an enjoyable pastime. The time was right for serious researchers to explore the sexual difficulties many people reported, and Masters and Johnson took up the challenge.

One of their major starting points was to discredit the long-held view that sexual problems are always a symptom of deep, underlying psychiatric illness that can be cured only by long-term psychotherapy. Instead, they claimed an impressive cure rate with their treatment program, which combined sex education, a series of couples exercises called Sensate Focus, and specific behavioral strategies for each of the sexual dysfunctions. This approach came to be known as sex therapy.

Sex therapy challenged old beliefs and lack of knowledge. It came as a surprise to many that women were capable of orgasm and that it was most likely achieved by clitoral rather than vaginal stimulation. Couples learned that what happened prior to intercourse (foreplay) was as important as the act itself. Men learned that they could delay ejaculation to enhance the satisfaction of both partners and that they didn't have to endure impotence in painful, embarrassed silence.

One of Masters and Johnson's most fundamental aims was to abolish goal-oriented performance. They believed that if people stopped being anxious about their performance and were willing to put into practice some basic techniques, good sex would happen naturally, making sexual pleasure within easy reach of everyone. (Interestingly, early sex therapy did not address the problem of sex drive: It was assumed that once a couple stopped being anxious about sex and learned how to achieve sexual pleasure, sex drive would automatically increase.)

As a young sex therapist in the early 1970s, I remember embracing all this exciting knowledge and the associated treatment protocols with an almost evangelical zeal. It seemed, back then, that sexual liberation was about to be realized—and my colleagues and I often joked that we'd be working ourselves out of a job, because there would be no need for sex therapists in the new millennium.

THE IRONY OF IT ALL

Despite 30 years of access to sex therapy and an increasing openness about sex during that time, the reported rates of sexual problems have not changed significantly—making for an interesting paradox. There's more sexual content in books and films than ever before, and there are hundreds of books and magazine articles dedicated to exploring and offering solutions for all kinds of sexual difficulties. In spite of this, a large survey of the US population conducted in 1994 by University of Chicago sociologist Edward Laumann, Ph.D., and his associates estimated that 43 percent of women and 31 percent of men in the United States have sexual problems. One in three women rated themselves as lacking interest in sex, which was double the reported rate for men. These figures are very similar to those of a UK-based study from 1998, which found that 41 percent of women and 34 percent of men had some form of sexual problem.

These results were astounding, particularly the figures on low sex drive in women. Although other more recent studies haven't found the same high rates, they still report that 20 percent of women, or one in five, complain of low libido. These numbers don't come as a surprise to sex therapists. Our offices are busy with women of all ages who worry because they don't feel like having sex as often as they believe they should, or as often as their partners would like.

Think about it. Sit in a mall and watch the crowds go by, and consider that at least one of every five women walking past you is likely to not be too keen on sex. That's an awful lot of worried or dissatisfied women and stressed relationships.

How did this happen? In an age of sexual sophistication and celebration of sexuality, when one of the best-selling books in the late 20th century was called *The Joy of Sex*, what went wrong? Why has all of the optimism we sex therapists had in the 1970s failed to be vindicated? Why, in particular, do so many women not want sex?

These are the questions the first part of this book seeks to answer. (And although I am focusing here specifically on women's lack of sexual interest, this isn't to say that men don't have their own problems. Indeed, one in six men in Dr. Laumann's 1994 study rated themselves as having little or no interest in sex, but in my clinical experience, the issues affecting male libido are different from those of concern to women, and they would justify a book of their own.)

This book is not about a mystical philosophy to put your sex life on a higher plane. It's not a guide to sexual positions and a variety of sexual techniques nor a manual of behavior programs to help you learn to be orgasmic or deal with painful intercourse. There are hundreds of books already available on these topics. Rather, it's a book for women—and their partners—who often feel irritated at the thought of sex or find they simply can't be bothered, then worry that there must be something wrong with them or their relationship. You'll be relieved to learn that this isn't necessarily the case.

To solve the problem, though, we have to start trying to see through a well-constructed illusion, which is the focus of the next chapter.

CHAPTER 2

CREATING AN ILLUSION

HOW DO WE KNOW WHAT GOOD SEX IS? We've certainly had a very long time to work out what it *should* be. According to anthropologist Edgar Gregersen, Ph.D., in his book, *Sexual Practices: The Story of Human Sexuality,* sex began more than 2,000,000,000 years ago. All life depends on it, and most people engage in some sort of sexual activity during their lifetime. Thus, you'd think it would be safe to assume that we would know all there is to know about a behavior that is so basic, so universal, so ancient. A few thousand years should be more than enough time to sort out any problems there might be about sex and discover the mysteries of sexual pleasure.

Yet, clearly, this isn't the case.

Certainly, we know a lot about the reproductive aspects of sex. Control of fertility and treatment programs for infertility were some of the most significant medical advances of the 20th century. Sex researchers have examined sexual behavior from every angle and by almost every means, from massive surveys to laboratory observations of people engaging in sexual acts.

So if we know so much about sex, why does it still cause us so many problems? Why do so many people feel inadequate and distressed about sexual issues?

The answer to these questions lies in the significance we attach to sexual behavior. The specific behaviors that are considered normal and adequate are influenced by prevailing sexual attitudes, and attitudes toward all behaviors, such as masturbation, premarital sex, homosexuality, and even female pleasure, vary around the world.

It's obvious from the people who consult me, as a sex therapist, that there are strong beliefs in Western society, as in all cultures, about what is normal and healthy. These clients are usually quite convinced that there is something wrong with them or their partner because they perceive that certain things essential to a good sex life are missing. To arrive at this conclusion, they must be comparing themselves with a model of normal, desirable sexual behavior.

Generally, the model that dominates in society at any given time is accepted as the one most likely to be correct, so if someone is different from what is expected, it is assumed that the problem lies with the person, not the set of beliefs. Although there are always groups in any society who disagree with majority opinions, whether more conservative or more radical, this specific view of what's considered normal is quite pervasive and influential. For example, societies still exist in which most people believe that female sexual pleasure is abhorrent, so the clitoris is routinely removed. At the same time, there are other societies in which most people believe that female pleasure is essential to a healthy sexual relationship. Individuals living in these cultures would have opposite views of normal and appropriate female sexual response simply because of the time and place in which they were born.

When people compare themselves with what's considered normal in society, they make judgments about themselves. Some may feel they are close enough to the standard to feel that they and/or their relationship is able to cope with any differences, but others seem to judge themselves quite harshly. Does this mean we are a society full of people who are inadequate, or does it mean that we are holding ourselves to an inappropriate standard?

TODAY'S SEXUAL STANDARDS

In the space of 50 years, Western society has passed through an amazing period of dramatic social change. In the 1950s, a person was expected to have only one lover in a lifetime; oral sex (and anal sex) was not only a sin but was illegal in many states; premarital pregnancy was a cause of deep shame, and most out-of-wedlock babies were given up for adoption; extramarital sex made the participants social outcasts; and nice girls, if they had orgasms, did it only one way, and certainly not through masturbation. We have now moved to a time in which casual sex is regarded as mundane, oral sex is essential, *not* having premarital sex is unusual, extramarital affairs are so common that we are bored with hearing about them, and women should have orgasms any which way they can.

How did that happen?

We saw in chapter 1 that by the 1960s, improved contraception meant that couples could focus more on sex for pleasure instead of worrying about unplanned pregnancies. In addition, the women's movement meant that women increasingly recognized that their needs were as important as men's. These developments stirred the winds of change that had begun to blow some years before, due in part to the publication of the work of sex researcher Alfred Kinsey, Ph.D., in the late 1940s and early 1950s. Dr. Kinsey studied the sexual behavior of children, and his report created much discussion and public controversy. Just as important, his results suggested that what people did in the privacy of their own home in terms of sex was often quite different from what was dictated by society.

The other social change that played a significant role in the sexualization of society was the evolution of mass media. Mass production of cheap paperbacks made books more accessible to the general population, the film industry grew throughout the century, and television brought stories of fact and fiction into people's living room.

The scientific research of Masters and Johnson provided legitimacy to the liberalization process and led to a rapid acceleration in the rate of change. Although their results seem so ordinary now, the impact of their research was startling at the time. In particular, they completely redefined the debate about female sexuality. It was no longer a question of whether women were capable of having a sexual response but rather of what kind of stimulation was most effective to bring a woman to orgasm—and perhaps many orgasms. They quickly demolished the debate about vaginal versus clitoral orgasm, declaring unequivocally that the center of excitement for women was the clitoris and that vaginal orgasms were merely a variation on that norm.

Some of their suggested treatment strategies provoked extreme outrage from both the general public and professional colleagues. One of the most radical techniques was to suggest that nonorgasmic women should be encouraged to masturbate, challenging centuries of disapproval and revulsion. Of particular significance was the revolutionary conclusion that love may not be enough to lead to sexual fulfillment and that varied techniques and a willingness to experiment were usually required to reach full sexual potential. Also, their original definition of premature ejaculation, which they stated was the inability of a man to delay ejaculation long enough to bring his partner to climax at least 50 percent of the time, focused attention on the need for men to be aware of women's enjoyment.

All of these changes together provided fertile ground for the shift from the belief that sex should be confined to marriage and be only about love to the idea that was, unwittingly perhaps, hidden in the work of Masters and Johnson—that sex is about knowledge, technique, and behavior. Their book *Human Sexual Inadequacy* seemed to provide a behavioral recipe for sexual pleasure, a "follow the steps" technique that was assumed to be achievable by everyone.

We took these ideas and ran with them. From this period in the 1970s, there was an ever-expanding market for sex manuals and self-help books for sexual problems, which were always described in behavioral terms: lack of orgasm, lack of erection, lack of ejaculatory control, inability to allow penetration, and, eventually, lack of sex drive.

Popular books such as Alex Comfort's *The Joy of Sex* (published in 1972) provided detailed and explicit answers to many questions we had about sex, and some we hadn't even thought of. Significant in terms of moving society from repressive ignorance to enlightened pleasure, Comfort's book set the standard for those that followed in the next couple of decades. He declared that mature, sophisticated, with-it couples want sex often, enjoy experimentation, and, if they followed his recipe, would, over time, learn how to have "cordon bleu" sex.

Thus began the creation of an illusion—a sexual illusion that was highly seductive. It promoted the ideas that good sex was an intensely physical experience that relied more on the right behaviors than on the quality of the emotional experience and that following the right behavioral formula could put this good sex within the reach of everyone.

There were many health professionals who helped construct this illusion. In 1980, psychologist Irene Kassorla, Ph.D., wrote that all a woman had to do was to follow the principles of the "pleasure process" and she could have 101 orgasms whenever she wanted them. In 1985, Dr. Theresa Larsen Crenshaw, detailed "how to have an orgasm whether you want one or not." Psychiatrist Dr. Alan Brauer, and his wife, counselor Donna Brauer, outlined a program in their 1984 book *Extended Sexual Orgasm* that promised "deep, continuous orgasm" and "intense pleasure" lasting 30 minutes to an hour or more.

When professional counselors eventually returned to the notion that the quality of the emotional relationship was usually a significant factor in creating a satisfying sex life, advice on communication skills, conflict resolution, and acceptance of each other became a standard feature of the new wave of sex manuals. This was not necessarily a bad thing, but authors promised that if you followed their advice to sort out your relationship issues *and* applied the right sexual techniques, your sex life would soar.

A more complex version of this type of self-help book for sexual problems was *Passionate Marriage*, by psychologist David Schnarch, Ph.D., which came out in 1997. Dr. Schnarch outlined his process of individual differentiation, in which both partners stay true to themselves and ultimately learn to give and take in a mature way in their sexual relationship. The experience of "wall-socket sex" is the reward for those couples who can successfully negotiate their way through this complex and difficult process.

POOR ADVICE ADDS TO THE MISERY

The following "advice" given to a reader of a magazine aimed at young women is a stark example of the role that some sex therapists, psychologists, and other professionals play in setting rigid and unrealistic standards for normal sexual behavior.

Q. Two weeks ago, during foreplay, my boyfriend asked me to watch him masturbate. I was shocked, and snapped, "No way, that's sick!" I told him to pleasure himself in private, not in front of me. He became angry and called me a prude. We haven't made love— or even spoken to each other—since that night. I can do without sex, but I miss the other parts of our relationship, and I fear this argument could harm it.

A. There's nothing unhealthy about your boyfriend's request: Many couples include masturbation in their erotic repertoires. Self-stimulation is a problem only if it replaces all other forms of sexual activity. I think your refusal to even consider indulging his fantasy signals that you have deeper emotional conflicts. Perhaps you feel guilty about your own sexual desire, or maybe you're afraid he no longer finds you attractive. You must determine why you're incapable of sharing an uninhibited sex life with your partner—perhaps by starting with a visit to a counselor?

The Media's Role: Fantasy vs. Reality

As I mentioned earlier in this chapter, the notion that explosive sex is the achievable norm has been regularly reinforced by the media. We have moved from the sexually bland movies of the 1950s, in which Doris Day and Rock Hudson played out their courtship in glorious Technicolor and innocent embraces, through the more suggestive brash sexuality of James Bond movies, to *Last Tango in Paris*, and finally, to now, when raunchy sex scenes are almost mandatory in most films.

Think of any movie of the past 20 years that has a sexual theme. How is sex portrayed? We see beautiful photography, naked bodies entwining, breasts being licked and nibbled, backs being stroked, deep-throat kissing, heightened arousal, and powerful orgasms, usually by penis–vagina contact that seems to last a very long time.

We don't see women requiring 15 minutes or more of clitoral stimulation to come to orgasm, women enjoying sex without orgasm, men coming quickly, men not being able to attain erections or penetrate the vagina without their partner's assistance, or anyone saying that he or she doesn't like what's being done, as in "I don't like you sucking my breasts," or "the thought of oral sex turns my stomach." In fact, any communication about sexual wants and needs is usually missing because it would not enhance the story or make it more exciting.

Realism in the movies is considered boring—and that's just the point. Sex as portrayed in them is fantasy, not reality. When we see Superman flying, we don't expect to fly as well, because we know that what we're seeing is fantasy. When it comes to sex, though, we seem to have fallen for the fantasy hook, line, and sinker.

The development of mass media, including novels, films, and television, meant that for the first time in history, stories of adventure, romance, and amazing exploits were presented to the general population in an increasingly realistic (which is not the same as *real*) way. These developments have saturated us with powerfully presented tales of fiction to the point where they form part of our everyday lives. How many sexual acts has a person seen portrayed by the age of 20? Over a lifetime? When you think about it, it would be hard *not* to be influenced by this exposure. After all, who wouldn't want to try to reach out and experience the delights of the intense sexual encounters that seem so tantalizingly real?

ACCOUNTING FOR THE PARADOX

I have no doubt that some of you will disagree with my assertion that hoping for explosive sex, at least on any sort of regular basis, suggests that you have fallen for an illusion. Surely, you may think, it's only reasonable to expect sex to be passionate and intense. Experimenting with a variety of techniques, positions, or whatever is the only way to keep sex exciting and fulfilling. It's ridiculous to think of settling for less!

So how do we account for the paradox of so many sexually unhappy people in a time of such openness and acceptance? Aren't we living in an era of tolerance, when individual differences are encouraged and diversity is accepted? People are now encouraged to understand themselves, to seek answers to the question, Who am I? and to find ways of fulfilling their individual potential. How can this be bad?

Suppose the answers to the question, Who am I? led to the conclusions, I'm not really that interested in sex, or, I don't mind sex now and again if it doesn't go on too long but all that acrobatic stuff just isn't for me? If the person who had those thoughts was in a relationship that was generally pretty good, but the other partner was keen on sex, liked to do it frequently, and really didn't think it was good sex unless it went on for a while and involved different techniques and positions, what judgments would the couple make of themselves and each other? Which partner would be more likely to be regarded as the "normal" one, and which would be more likely to take responsibility for problems in the sexual relationship and seek counseling?

What is often overlooked in any discussions of what is normal is how diverse we all are and the resilience of this diversity. In any society at any time, there are always people who don't conform to what is considered normal, no matter how strong the pressure is to do so.

Ironically, this means that some people who would have believed they were sexually deviant and damned forever 100 years ago would now regard themselves as perfectly normal and be accepted by others as such, perhaps boringly so. There were at that time, despite the strong prohibitions against it, many children and adults who masturbated, many people who had premarital sex or extramarital affairs, and many couples who enjoyed a variety of sexual activities. The difference is that then, these behaviors often caused people great distress. There are records of young adults who felt such despair that they wanted to commit suicide because of their desire to masturbate. In the 1940s, Ingrid Bergman was ostracized and fled the United States because she became pregnant as a result of an affair with film director Roberto Rossellini.

Although societal stereotypes about normal and acceptable behaviors do have a strong influence on what people actually do, their greatest impact is on what people believe and how this affects their sexual self-esteem. Because sexuality cannot be rigidly defined and confined, there will always be people who simply cannot fit into the accepted norms of the time. The end results for these people are usually feelings of inadequacy, guilt, perversion, and often despair.

In today's world, ironically, the people who feel this way aren't those who are pushing the moral boundaries and exploring new and diverse sexual behaviors. Instead, the people who wonder if there is something wrong with them are those who prefer to stay on the quiet side of sexuality and who may not rank sex as a high priority. Therefore, in reality, although we pride ourselves on being sexually sophisticated and open-minded, we have as limited a view of sexual diversity as people did at any earlier time in history.

In the following chapters, we will see that despite paying lip service to individual differences and differences between the sexes, there is much we choose to ignore. As a result, too many people are being led to believe that they have sexual problems when they are in fact perfectly normal. What's more, the emphasis on the belief that what we do in a sexual encounter creates the meaning and emotional importance of that encounter, rather than the other way around, causes many individuals and couples unnecessary anguish.

As we explore these issues, we will begin to understand why there are so many women who aren't interested in sex.

CHAPTER 3

THE FORGOTTEN INDIVIDUAL

ALL SOCIETIES DEVELOP MODELS OF NORMAL AND ACCEPTABLE BEHAVIOR, and people are often judged according to those standards. In some cultures, conformity to the norms is expressly encouraged, and deviations are punished—sometimes brutally. In Western society, we believe we recognize that people are individuals, that not everyone can be the same, and that each person has value for his particular characteristics.

Yet the truth is that we are more comfortable with conformity. For example, even though a rebellious teenager may reject the values of his parents, he will willingly conform to the attitudes and values of his peers. Being too different is to risk social rejection—a fact of life that persists across all levels of our society. We adopt the fashion, the language, and the rituals of our peer groups, finding comfort and strength in this common understanding of the way things should be.

Although there's no doubt that sometimes individuality is prized— usually when someone has an admired or acquired quality that sets him apart from others, such as musical talent or a brilliant mind—we often scorn those we perceive as different in other, more circumstantial ways, such as race, religion, language, or social customs. We have stereotypes about the ideal figure, the good mother, the manly male—so many standards by which we judge ourselves or others negatively. The lack of confidence to be yourself is amazingly pervasive in our supposedly self-aware society.

THE ILLUSION OF SEXUAL INDIVIDUALITY

Sexually, we like to think that we have it together, that we are more sophisticated and sexually aware now than at any other time in history. Yet, as we have seen, the current stereotype of normal, desirable sex is still quite narrow and rigid.

One exercise I often do when training sex therapists involves asking them to describe what normal sexual frequency is. Typically, the answer is, Whatever is right for the individual. Then I ask how they would describe someone who only rarely desires sex, or a couple where one partner wants sex twice a week and the other once a month. Is one person closer to "normal" than the other? How would they, as sex therapists, go about helping this couple achieve sexual harmony? Which person is under more pressure to change? Despite the standard answer from therapists that this couple suffers from mismatched libidos and that both people are "normal," the pressure in therapy is most commonly on the person with the lower sex drive to pick up the pace.

When people claim to be liberated sexually, what they really mean is that they explore and enjoy experimentation and variety at the active, lusty, passionate end of the scale. We feel we are being broad-minded when we are comfortable with or tolerant of sexual diversity, such as homosexuality or bisexuality, or are prepared to experiment with oral sex, sex toys, threesomes, or bondage and discipline.

However, if we are to truly embrace the notion of individual differences in sexuality, we need to think far more broadly than this and become respectful of people who are at the other end of the spectrum. Where does the asexual individual fit into the scheme of things? How is a person who prefers only "conventional" sex judged? What label is given to someone who is turned off by oral sex or by being touched on the genitals? What words are used to describe a woman—or man—who doesn't seem interested in sex? What are some of the factors that are commonly thought to lead to this disinterest?

In a recent survey in the United States, 43 percent of women and 31 percent of men identified themselves as having one or more sexual problems. Among women, 33 percent complained of low sexual desire, 24 percent reported inability to come to orgasm, and 14 percent stated they experience pain during sex. For men, the most frequently reported problem was premature ejaculation, accounting for 28 percent of complaints, while 15 percent rated themselves as lacking interest in sex, 10 percent said they had problems attaining or maintaining an erection, and 3 percent had physical pain during intercourse.

Some researchers have criticized this study because these problems were identified by self-rating rather than by clinical evaluation, but it is precisely this aspect of the survey that intrigues me. If one in three women believes she is not as interested in sex as she should be, and one in four men doesn't last as long as he thinks he should last, which of the following is more likely?

- We have a major epidemic on our hands.
- Many in this self-selected group aren't dysfunctional at all but are either variations on the norm or comparing themselves unrealistically with an ideal.

It's difficult to believe that such a large proportion of our population is sexually inadequate. Because problems such as painful intercourse and difficult erections are relatively objective, the figures given are likely to be fairly accurate, but even within these categories, the problems may be caused by worry about performance rather than by any psychological or physical disorder.

Many women who believe they are not experiencing arousal and orgasm have been influenced by the stereotype of hot and powerful sexual response portrayed in the media and promoted by the myth that if you aren't sure whether you've had an orgasm, you haven't! Some women who believe they are unable to reach orgasm are surprised to learn that that nice warm feeling or that sigh of relaxation is an orgasm, even if it is perhaps a 2 on a 10-point scale.

Concerns about sexual desire and ejaculatory control can be more subjectively determined and evaluated. What is sexual desire? Is it physical passion, or is it an emotional desire for intimacy? Can it be different things at different times? Is it possible to want sex but prefer to avoid it, and if so, why? What is a "normal" level of sexual interest?

Interestingly, this survey did not include questions about desiring sex with great frequency. Does that mean that you can't want sex too much, but you can want it too little?

How quick is too quick for ejaculation? Which partner is worried about it? Why? Is the problem that the woman finds it difficult to come to orgasm with penile thrusting despite the man controlling ejaculation for a reasonable time?

Additionally, for those people who rated themselves as *not* having problems, how did they decide this? Were all of them behaving close to the cultural norm, or were some of them confident enough to be happy to be different?

These questions need to be carefully considered before anyone, including sex therapists and researchers, can begin to understand the extent of individual variation in sexuality. Until these issues are thoroughly explored and discussed in sex manuals, magazine articles, and self-help books, people in the community will continue to rate themselves as having sexual problems even when there's a good chance that they're perfectly normal.

Normal Variation in Individual Sexuality

Thirty years as a sex therapist has highlighted for me what should be recognized as a self-evident truth—that people are not the same sexually, in the same way that they are not the same with respect to height, weight, intelligence, personality, food preferences, general health, and so on. In spite of the fact that the many ways in which people differ sexually become evident from just listening to them talk about their sexual experiences, there is little or no discussion of such differences by authors writing in the field of human sexuality. There are the acknowledged differences in sexual orientation, but gay and lesbian couples can also find it difficult to negotiate differences in individual wants and needs.

One of the most obvious ways in which people differ is in terms of their interest in sex, usually called sex drive. However, there are several other characteristics that also vary among individuals, as evident from the following list.

Frequency of sexual activity. Some people hope for, keenly want, or desperately need sexual activity several times a week or perhaps even more than once a day, whereas others are entirely satisfied to have sex once a month or even less often. Although there is general acceptance that the need for sex varies, there is no agreement as to what, if anything, constitutes an abnormally low or abnormally high sex drive. It's easy to see, however, that there would be some tension in a relationship where one person wants sex several times a week and the other would like it less than once a month.

Robustness of desire. Fluctuation of interest is a specific aspect of sex drive that can be confusing. Some people's level of interest remains reasonably constant no matter what else is happening in their lives, whereas others may switch off if they feel overwhelmed by other issues. This can lead to misinterpretation of motives: A person whose interest stays steady regardless of life events may seem insensitive, while one whose desire fluctuates may sometimes seem emotionally less committed to the other partner.

Type of desire. Currently, the expectation in Western culture is that sex drive is about hot passion or physical lust, but for some people, desire is much more muted and may be softly emotional rather than intensely physical. How does one partner interpret the signals of the other?

Desire versus response. This difference has been recognized in sex research for many years, but it doesn't seem to be widely appreciated in the community. There are some people who want to engage in sexual activity quite frequently but who may not become aroused and orgasmic.

Conversely, there are many people who aren't aware of any regular interest in sex and feel they could live without it, but if the partner initiates sex under the right circumstances, they can respond with enthusiasm.

Initiation versus response. It makes sense that if someone rarely feels the desire for sex even though she may enjoy it when it occurs, she isn't likely to initiate it very often. It simply doesn't occur to her, and her partner may be devastated, seeing it as a rejection or an indication that he's not sexually attractive. An imbalance in frequency of initiation of sex can be a major hurdle for couples to overcome.

Ease of arousal. Some people find it difficult to get turned on, and their partner complains that it takes a lot of work to start to get them hot, while other people respond quickly. Sometimes, those who are slow to arouse are not confident enough to say what they need, or their partner persists in trying to stimulate them in various ways that actually turn them off. Nevertheless, the bottom line is that some people simply arouse more quickly than others.

Time to orgasm. Why do some people come more quickly than others? Should everyone be able to reach orgasm in a standard period of time? There are behavioral programs that can teach men who ejaculate rapidly how to delay reaching orgasm and that can help those with inhibited ejaculation come more easily, and there are strategies that will help women become aroused and come to orgasm more quickly. However, there will still be a range of times that it takes to come to orgasm, with some people having characteristic patterns of early (easy) or late (difficult) orgasm and others varying widely, depending on the circumstances.

Variation in response style. Perhaps this variable would be better termed variation in pleasure style. Sometimes, one partner has little interest in sex and doesn't really want to become aroused and have an orgasm, being quite happy to have quiet, cuddly sex, while at other times, the physical response is strong and urgent. This can be confusing if the other partner thinks sex is always about arousal, experimentation, and so on. And, of course, there are individuals who mostly prefer quiet intimacy and find attempts at sexual arousal irritating, which can leave both partners bewildered and frustrated.

Variety in sexual behaviors. There seems to be an almost limitless range of things that people can do for sexual pleasure. Titles of magazine articles such as "1,001 Ways to Drive Your Man Wild in Bed" give some idea of the smorgasbord that's available. However, it would be unreasonable to expect all people to like all of these behaviors. There are those who find particular acts abhorrent and those who find them simply boring. Some people prefer to rely on a limited number of tried-and-true activities, while others crave variety and experimentation.

Importance of sex. People's responses differ significantly when they're asked to rank the importance of sex in a relationship when compared with other variables, such as love, affection, companionship, financial security, children, and so on. Although studies consistently show that men tend to rate sex as more important than women do, this is a generalization, and either gender may give sex a high or low priority.

These are some of the variations in human sexuality that I have encountered in my long practice of sex therapy. I don't know how the normal/abnormal boundaries should be set, but it's my view that most of this variation should be considered part of normal human diversity.

Does this mean we must just accept how we are and not try to reach goals that may make sex more satisfying or relationships easier? If not, how do we decide what can be changed, and by what method? These are not easy questions to answer.

Certainly, sexual problems exist. If people believe they have a problem, then clearly something is worrying them. However, if they are comparing themselves with an unattainable ideal, their individual level of sexual functioning is not validated, and what is normal for them becomes defined as sexual dysfunction. The real problem confronting us is how to decide if someone's concern is a matter of definition and misinformation or if the behavior is truly outside the normal range. Even if it's not common, does this make it a dysfunction?

SEXUAL POTENTIAL: NOT CREATED EQUAL

Lack of acceptance of the extent of individual differences, and the associated belief that normal people experience regular sexual desire and enjoy experimentation, has led to the belief that everyone has the same sexual potential. Surely, the thinking goes, if it's normal to have a persistent physical sex drive, for example, there must be some way to help people who don't have it to overcome their problem. The idea that what many people are already doing may be the best they can do is just not acceptable. It's this assumption that has caused so much misery in our time.

The emergence of sex therapy in the 1970s encouraged the view that everyone has the same sexual potential. Behavioral programs to teach women to be orgasmic and men to delay ejaculation assumed that with the right strategies, everyone could achieve these goals. If these programs didn't work for some people, the usual conclusion was that they were suffering from some form of sexual pathology that was loosely labeled sexual inhibition. The logical conclusion that perhaps the particular goals or techniques weren't right for those people wasn't even discussed. Although sex therapy has undergone many shifts in recent times, the idea that there may be many definitions of a successful sexual relationship is still not usually addressed by either therapists or clients.

Instead, we have spent a lot of energy trying to identify the factors associated with sexual "failure." A common view is that if we "fail" sexually, there must be some sexual trauma or secret in our past to account for it and that not reaching the standard is inevitably bad and should be corrected with therapy.

Sexual Personalities

Look around at your friends, family, and colleagues. Each person has a unique set of behaviors, thoughts, and feelings that make up the sum of whom they are. This set of characteristics forms the personality of the

EFFECTS OF PAST TRAUMA

We have become preoccupied with dwelling on the past, exploring it in minute and emotional detail, to uncover why we fail to be whom we want to be. Although everyone has a past made up of good and bad experiences, that doesn't mean it's inevitable that exposure to trauma will have long-term adverse effects. Even if past traumas do have continuing impact, they're not necessarily responsible for *all* of the problems we may have as adults.

This issue is an important one to reflect on because the failure to perform sexually according to cultural stereotypes (i.e., the diagnosis of sexual dysfunction) and the belief that this is caused by a traumatic past—specifically childhood sexual abuse—have become intricately linked in current thinking. Yet the research on long-term effects of sexual abuse consistently demonstrates a wide range of reactions into adulthood, with most victims ultimately developing into well-functioning adults.

Thus, there is no clear-cut, inevitable association between childhood sexual abuse and adult sexual problems. It certainly isn't helpful when therapists make sweeping generalizations about victims of childhood trauma generally developing issues with trust, or when they focus more therapy time on a history of abuse if a woman lacks a strong libido, rather than giving equal weight to other issues, such as the couple's unrealistic sexual expectations. There's no doubt that sexual abuse is a disgusting crime, but there are many factors that influence its long-term effects. Everyone needs to be treated with respect and supported in their individual reactions.

individual and is consistently present for that person. Some characteristics may dominate or be present in all interactions, while others may reveal themselves only in specific situations.

In general, personality is considered to be stable over a person's lifetime, but not all characteristics are fixed or inflexible, and people can and do adapt according to circumstances and life experiences.

At the present time, there is a tendency to use sexual personality characteristics in a critical way. For example, for "conservative," read "inhibited"; for "shy," read "hung up"; and so on. However, if we acknowledge that each person has a unique personality and that what one person likes and admires in a friend, another may find annoying, then we can assume that the situation is similar with sexual personalities. In other words, what one person finds attractive, endearing, or exciting in someone else's sexual personality may be a complete turnoff for a different person.

Who is in a position to make a judgment as to which personality is the most functional? In the end, this judgment tends to become relevant only when an individual becomes involved in a sexual interaction. Of course, this brings into play the importance of the relationship between the two: A relationship characterized by mutual generosity, kindness, and gentleness is more likely to be able to resolve or accommodate differences than is one that is harsh, critical, and rigid.

SETTING INDIVIDUAL GOALS

From the preceding discussion, we can begin to understand that sex therapy cannot be a simple matter of identifying a symptom and applying a behavioral formula, nor is there a need to always engage in deep and meaningful analysis of hidden blocks and inhibitions. Sorting out what is an achievable and realistic goal for an individual or a couple has to take into account each person's biological, psychological, and social influences and help them discover their own sexual potential.

Sex therapy, then, has three possible goals: to improve actual sexual performance, to change clients' attitudes about what they are already doing, or a combination of both. Certainly, a change in techniques can possibly develop orgasmic response in some women or help some men control ejaculation. By expanding sexual knowledge and technique, frequency of sex can be increased for some couples in which one partner wants it much less than the other. However, if the clients' current situation is already as good as it's going to be, therapy is aimed at helping them enjoy what they are already doing, rather than worrying about what they aren't.

In attempting to resolve stresses caused by individual differences in sexual needs and wants, it's important not to lose sight of the fact that there are two people making up the partnership. One person does not have more rights than the other does in the relationship. If each partner has different wants and needs, it's not surprising that sometimes conflict or disappointment occurs, but one person is not more entitled than the other is to have his or her sexual values determine the course of the sexual relationship.

Although individual differences undoubtedly play a role in the sexual difficulties of many couples, they can't completely explain why lack of interest in sex occurs more often with women than with men. Now we need to venture into the controversial debate about similarities and differences between the sexes.

CHAPTER 4

ARE THE SEXES *REALLY* DIFFERENT?

THERE WAS A TIME DURING THE LATE 20TH CENTURY when it was politically incorrect to even suggest that there might be innate behavior differences between the sexes. Girls grew up to be nurturing because they played with dolls and weren't allowed to play with trucks; boys grew up to be competitive because they played with guns and were teased if they played "sissy" games. Any differences that were noticed were thought to be due to this type of social conditioning.

This gender stereotyping extended into the sexual area as well. The challenge thrown down to traditional gender stereotypes in the 1960s by the emerging women's movement meant that female sexuality was also headed for a dramatic reevaluation. As I noted in chapter 1, this process was aided by the work of influential sex researchers Masters and Johnson.

In hindsight, it seems to be a fair assumption that sex research during that period was likely to be shaped, however subtly, by the ideological debates of the time. Masters and Johnson, whose radical research included laboratory observation of individuals engaged in masturbation and couples performing intercourse, concluded that the response cycles of the sexes were remarkably similar and that the similarities between the sexes far outweighed the differences. This meant that they chose to downplay differences such as the effect of fatigue or stress on time to orgasm (men under stress tend to come more quickly, whereas women under stress take longer to reach orgasm). However, differences such as these can in fact play a significant role in the sexual relationship between a man and woman.

Sex therapists took the lead from Masters and Johnson and generally accounted for gender dissimilarities in sexual behavior in terms of learned responses due to differences in upbringing. It's common, for example, for a sexual problem to be described by a couple as the man's belief that they don't have enough sex, along with the woman's belief is that there isn't enough affection. This issue is usually included in discussions of relationship problems and is most commonly explained in terms of early upbringing and the pressure of gender role expectations. The traditional view held by writers in the past century that this reflects the natural order of male/female differences had been abandoned.

In general, it was believed that women were raised to deny their sexuality, so that problems such as low sex drive or difficulty achieving orgasm occurred because they had not been taught to explore their sexuality and develop their full sexual potential. The implicit assumption was that if this situation were changed, men and women would be more evenly matched. In 1985, psychologist Irene Kassorla, Ph.D., took a somewhat more extreme view to promote repressed female abilities when she expounded her belief that all women were capable of 101 orgasms whenever they wanted and that they were failing to reach this potential only because of the pressure of societal stereotypes.

It is interesting to recognize now that in challenging gender differences, the conclusion that was typically drawn by the experts was that the male stereotype of the importance of sex, persistent sex drive, easy arousal, need for orgasm, and desire to experiment *was the correct one.* This stereotype excluded the notion that it is also perfectly normal for a male not to feel that sex is important, to have low libido, to not need orgasm during sexual activity, and to prefer quiet, brief sexual sessions (ideas we'll explore further in the next chapter).

Although in my view, sex therapists were often biased by their own values as they tried to deal with the thorny problem of differences between male and female sexuality, they nevertheless tried to discuss the issue in a considered and concerned way. In contrast, the mass media embraced the new version of female sexuality with unrestrained enthusiasm. Gone are the demure looks of Doris Day and the female wiles of Lucille Ball. Now, women are typically portrayed as highly sexual, even predatory, and certainly hotly passionate and easily aroused. Nonviolent erotica is particularly replete with the new stereotype of the lascivious woman who just can't get enough of hot sex. Yet even now, in the sexuality workshops I conduct, people still account for the sexual problems women experience in terms of repressive societal stereotypes.

All this effort to reduce any differences between women and men to differences in learning has ignored a very basic point: If we accept the notion that differences can be produced as a result of social conditioning, surely the converse is also true—that similarities can be shaped by social forces. Has this been part of the sexual revolution of the last few decades?

SOCIETY'S INFLUENCE

Behavior isn't all innate, nor is it all learned. Some differences in behavior are more biologically determined, some are learned, and some are shaped by a combination of the two forces. What's hard, of course, is identifying how much each of these factors contributes to specific behaviors—particularly those that are considered to be a problem and need to be changed.

There is no doubt that cultural values and expectations influence behavior. The field of cross-cultural psychology is full of fascinating examples of the impact of social norms on people's attitudes and behaviors. Studies have shown that variations across cultures occur in such

DO DIFFERENCES MATTER?

Does it really matter if there are innate differences between the sexes? If such differences exist, why not just treat them as one type of individual difference? For example, a woman finds orgasm more difficult to achieve when she is tired, but under the same circumstances, a man is more likely to come quickly. Is it necessary or useful to identify this as a general difference between the sexes rather than just deal with it as a difference between the two people in a relationship?

My answer to that argument, which is often put forward by people trying to deny or downplay gender differences, is that if there are biological influences that produce even subtle variations in sexual behavior, then recognizing and evaluating them is likely to be helpful in understanding an individual's sexual behavior. Understanding leads to greater confidence and increases the probability of reaching full sexual potential.

Consider the example of the contraceptive pill. Loss of interest in sex is a side effect of oral contraceptives for some women, but certainly not all women or even the majority of them. If a woman who complains of loss of sex drive is using the Pill, it would be irresponsible not to consider this in assessing her problem. It's not always easy to determine whether and to what extent it's a contributing factor, but a good therapist certainly would not dismiss it. Similarly, taking into account the possible impact of gender differences helps the therapist explore all potentially relevant issues.

diverse areas as problem-solving style, dream content and the ability to recall dreams, and even the age at which a child first walks. The physical environment, the knowledge base of the culture, religious beliefs, and so on all play a part in shaping what people think, believe, and do in any society.

This includes significant differences across cultures in sexual beliefs and behaviors. Definitions of sexual attractiveness; acceptability of specific sexual techniques, such as oral or anal sex; and patterns of premarital and extramarital relationships are only some of the areas of human sexuality that vary across societies. Views on the appropriate behavior for men and women vary as well, meaning that what is regarded as normal behavior for a man or a woman in one society may be regarded as bizarre or inhibited in another.

These examples demonstrate that some of the traditional differences in the sexual behavior of men and women in our society are likely to be the result of social conditioning. There are many layers to the socialization process that contribute to the psychosexual development of the child: family, peers, school, church, socioeconomic group, and the broader society, including the media.

Media Influences on Men and Women

There are some differences in the media influences on men and women. Women tend to prefer to read tales of erotic fiction, resulting in Mills and Boon (publisher of Harlequin Romances) being one of the largest publishing houses in the world. In contrast, men have a large industry of male-oriented magazines with the emphasis on erotic photographs vying for their attention. Indeed, men are constantly exposed to the nude female body in calendars, advertisements, and movies as well as sexually explicit magazines, whereas women tend not get the same opportunity to see the nude male body, particularly in an aroused state, during the most formative years in the development of their sexuality. This may help to explain differences in what men and women find attractive. Many women do not find the sight of naked men a powerful trigger for sexual arousal, while many men need only to imagine a woman undressing to feel sexually interested. This may also explain why men have an easier time having sexual fantasies, which may influence differences in the development of sexual desire.

There are countless magazine articles aimed at young, single women advising them how to be more sexual and perform sexual activities better. Where are the equivalent articles for young men? This can be a problem for both sexes—for women because, as we have seen, some of the advice is problematic, and for men because they are expected to know about sex without necessarily receiving much information beyond that gleaned from movies and girly magazines.

Paradoxically, widespread media portrayal of casual sexual activity as the norm for single women has led to a situation in which women who are reluctant to have sex early in a relationship can be labeled as frigid, yet calling a woman a whore or a slut is still a common insult. Interestingly, there's no equivalent insult for men. Although women may talk among themselves about a man they regard as a sleaze, this is rarely used as an insult to the man himself. In therapy, women often have regrets about having had numerous sexual partners, referring to themselves as promiscuous, whereas this seems to be an uncommon concern for men, who may in fact be proud of such a history.

So, just like women in the last century, women are given some very confusing mixed messages about sex—it's just that the emphasis has changed. For example, a woman should be quite willing to have sex on the first or second date, be sexually uninhibited and adventurous, and certainly be happy to give and receive oral sex. But then you have to wonder how easy she is if she does have sex so readily. Maybe she's a slut after all?

Although the situation isn't quite as bad for men, they are also subjected to conflicting pressures. There's the expectation that he has to be a sexual athlete, not let anxiety interfere with his performance early in a relationship, maintain an erection indefinitely, have exquisite control over ejaculation, and at the same time be sensitive and caring about the woman's needs and value emotional intimacy over sexual performance, or she will eventually leave him. It's clear that many of the messages both sexes receive from society do little to help them understand themselves and relate to each other.

HOW BIOLOGY INFLUENCES BEHAVIOR

Until recently, the suggestion that biological factors might have a significant influence on behavior was both political and academic heresy. This applied not only to differences in the behavior of the sexes but also to behavior in general. We seem to resent the notion that sometimes some of the things we do may be the result of following a script laid down by our distant ancestors rather than a product of wise choices or complex learning. For several decades, "nurture" appeared to have won the "nature/nurture" debate: Evolution may have led to the physical organism that human beings are today, but it was society and culture that created the person.

Then, during the late 20th century, notes of dissent began to be heard. They came first from the biological sciences but became a much stronger, albeit still controversial, voice in the 1990s, when the term *evolutionary psychology* came into use. According to evolutionary psychologists, millions of years of the evolutionary process have endowed the human species with a variety of preset behavioral options that help determine modern behavior. These psychologists do not claim that a certain set of behaviors is inevitable in a given situation but rather that because certain behaviors have been useful and contributed to the survival of the species in the past, these behaviors are more easily triggered than other options.

The idea that the sexes have been programmed differently by evolutionary forces has been translated into popular psychology by a number of authors, the most famous being John Gray, Ph.D., who began with *Men Are from Mars, Women Are from Venus* and expanded on the theme in subsequent books, such as *Mars and Venus in the Bedroom*. Though these books are dismissed by some as trading on outdated stereotypes, their phenomenal success indicates that they ring true for many people.

What is interesting from my reading of the evolutionary theorists is that there are two schools of thought about the nature of male and female sex drive. One theory states that men must have evolved with a higher sex drive because their biological imperative is to spread their genes as widely as possible but that women don't need to be as driven and must be more cautious and sparing in their sexual behavior. The other theory, supported by evolutionary anthropologist Helen Fisher, Ph.D., says that men and women both have strong sex drives but for different reasons: men to spread their genes, and women to acquire and keep resources to help them raise the few children they have. Women have developed two alternative strategies to achieve this: either to be faithful to one man whom they keep happy with regular sex in order to receive the benefits of his resources, or to try to acquire as many resources as possible from a variety of partners, permanent or otherwise. With either of these theories, you can draw the conclusion that the nature of male and female sex drive is likely to be different, even if both are equally motivated to have sex. This is consistent with the main theme we are exploring in this book.

SEXUAL PHYSIOLOGY: THE BIG PICTURE

The physiology of sexual functioning is mind-bogglingly complex. We still don't fully understand all the intricacies of the neural, hormonal, and vascular requirements of sexual performance. It was only as recently as 1998 that an Australian urological surgeon, Dr. Helen O'Connell, removed clitorises from female cadavers and discovered that the clitoris is much larger and the associated neural network of the female genitals is far more extensive than previously recognized.

This complexity leads to a great deal of disagreement among researchers about whether physiological differences between the sexes predispose men and women to differences in sexual expression.

The most common debate is about strength of sex drive and the role of hormones. The relationship between testosterone and sex drive in men seems well established: Men need a good level of testosterone in order to experience physical sex drive; abnormal or very low levels of testosterone are associated with low levels of sexual interest. However, within the normal range of testosterone, the relationship between the hormone and drive is less clear cut: A person with higher hormone levels may not necessarily have the highest sex drive. Other factors, such as the person's upbringing, can moderate the role of hormones.

For women, the picture is more confusing. To begin with, we don't know what causes physical desire in a woman. Researchers argue about whether testosterone, estrogen, or progesterone is the major hormone of drive for women, with increasing speculation about the role of oxytocin in female sexuality. If it is testosterone (which seems to be the favored contender), women have much lower levels than men do, so does this suggest that women are likely to experience lower levels of sex drive? The results of testosterone therapy for women have not really clarified the issue. It can help some women with low libido but only those with a low (female) level of testosterone, and these are usually women in the menopausal age range. Even then, probably only 50 percent benefit from this type of hormone replacement therapy.

This picture is even more blurry when we consider that maybe half of all women report that they experience changes in sexual interest over the course of their menstrual cycle (and just as many women experience no change), but there is no consistent picture of when the peak level of sexual interest occurs. Because the various hormones circulating through a woman peak at different times throughout the cycle, does this mean that some women respond more to the influence of one hormone and that others are more sensitive to another? Very confusing!

The argument that men have a stronger and more robust sex drive is supported by my clinical observation that it is rare to meet a man who has never at any stage in his life experienced physical desire, whereas many women report that they have never experienced even a flicker of spontaneous physical need for sex. It seems unlikely that this can be accounted for by personal history alone; like women, there are men who have had distressing lives, including traumatic sexual experiences. In addition, in couples in which it's the man who is less interested in sex with his partner, many of the men report ongoing sexual desire to which they respond with masturbation. More correctly, then, many men with low libido in fact have problems with avoidance of sex in the relationship (for many different reasons). In contrast, most women who don't want sex say that they can live without it, that they rarely think of sex or feel frustrated, and that it doesn't occur to them to masturbate.

It's also rare to meet a man who has never under any circumstances experienced ejaculation and the pleasure that accompanies it (i.e., orgasm). Certainly, there are men who note diminished orgasms, usually associated with stress of some kind, but such men typically have past histories of good orgasms. In contrast, it's quite common to meet women who have never had an orgasm, have one only rarely, or require much stimulation to reach orgasm.

There is an argument that orgasm is as integral to female sexuality as to male sexuality, because research has shown that female orgasm during intercourse facilitates conception. Here again, however, there is a major difference in function. Arousal and ejaculation, presumably accompanied by orgasm, are essential to conception, whereas it is certainly possible for a woman to be totally unaroused and still conceive.

These observations support the evolutionary theorists' conclusions that men and women are influenced by their genetic predisposition to behave in different ways under certain circumstances. Recognizing and understanding these tendencies may be helpful when trying to understand why so many women have difficulty in their sexual relationships.

Does Anatomy Make a Difference?

There are some physical features that obviously distinguish men and women. Can the fact that a man has a penis that penetrates, while a woman has a vagina that is entered influence sexuality in any meaningful way? This may seem to be a frivolous question, but to judge for yourself, imagine that you are the opposite sex, and picture yourself having intercourse. Do you think there would be any difference in your experience of sex? This is one you could argue about, but it seems reasonable to suspect that men and women do experience sex differently.

There is one way in which the differences in anatomy and sexual functioning do play a role in the motivation to have sex. Because women don't have to be aroused for intercourse to occur, and because it's easy for them to be passive during intercourse, they can choose to have sex or have it forced upon them under a variety of circumstances. Men have to be aroused and have a good erection for intercourse to be possible, so they generally need to be confident about their own ability to achieve this before they seek sex with a partner.

Anatomy does seem to play a role in at least one other aspect of sexual behavior: masturbation. This is significant because masturbation can play an important part in the development of sex drive as well as sexual response.

Men are more likely to masturbate than women are, and men who masturbate do so more often than women who masturbate. Though to some extent this reflects differences in cultural acceptance of male and female masturbation, men get more cues from their bodies to experiment with it.

To start with, at puberty, a young man *automatically* experiences sexual arousal that is focused on the genitals: The penis becomes erect (without any prompting at all), and ejaculation occurs, usually associated with orgasm. All this happens virtually in front of his eyes because his sexual organ is large and in a noticeable position. The size and position of his penis also mean that it receives frequent stimulation by such everyday activities as washing or by pressure of clothing, which can give strong clues to the pleasurable sensations to be achieved from conscious touch.

In contrast, the obvious thing that happens to a young girl at puberty is that she begins to menstruate, which is not usually associated with pleasurable feelings. Ovulation occurs quietly within the body and is usually unnoticed, even for girls who experience an increase in sexual interest at that time. The external female sex organs are small and hidden, and nothing obvious happens to draw a girl's attention to the pleasures that are possible. Therefore, though it doesn't take the average young man too long to realize that he can bring on those nice feelings of arousal and orgasm by self-stimulation, young women can be left in a sexual wilderness.

Masturbation is really sexual exercise: It aids the development of sex drive and sexual response. Just as important, it helps to develop the mind sexually. What do you think young boys are thinking of while they are stimulating their penises? Their math homework? A pleasant country scene? No, they are obviously playing out some wonderful sexual fantasy.

This gives men a decided advantage over women. It trains them to enjoy thinking about sex, it helps them to build sexual arousal and anticipate sexual activity, and it makes it easier for them to focus on pleasurable sexual feelings with a partner. This could partly explain why women are less likely to think about sex during the day, seem to take longer to become aroused, and are more distracted during sex than men are.

Two Other Differences

There are two more interesting observations about the sexes that may be linked to underlying physical differences.

The first is that women seem to vary more in what we might call the "everyday" area of sexuality. In other words, women seem to span evenly across the range of sex drive (from wanting sex daily or more often to not being bothered if they never had sex again); frequency of orgasm (from every sexual encounter to rarely or never); and ease of orgasm (from requiring minimal clitoral stimulation to needing prolonged stimulation). Men, on the other hand, seem more consistent as a group in terms of experiencing regular desire for sexual activity, and they usually desire and achieve orgasm relatively easily with erotic stimulation (although there is a type of sexual dysfunction known as inhibited ejaculation).

Women, however, vary less when it comes to less common sexual activities. Thus, there are significantly fewer female exhibitionists, cross-dressers, fetishists, and transsexuals. It's likely that because during adolescence men experience a more physically intense, genitally focused sexual desire, it's easier for them to develop a broad range of sexual fantasies that are reinforced by masturbation. For reasons we don't completely understand, some people's sexual fantasies incorporate unusual variations. I have seen men who are aroused by shoes, leather, plastic, bondage, near-asphyxia, animals—the list is almost endless—but I have seen very few women with these interests.

GENDER DIFFERENCES IN RELATIONSHIPS

Clinical experience and sex research projects report some interesting observations of how the differences in the sexual behavior of women and men affect the way they tend to behave in relationships.

One of the most enduring beliefs about differences between the sexes deals with the relationship between love and sex. As we saw in chapter 1, the importance of sex for women was traditionally tied to that of achieving motherhood. This led to the belief that women derived mainly emotional satisfaction from the act of sex, with little or no physical satisfaction, whereas men sought sex for its physical pleasures. This has often been translated into the mantra that women use sex in order to get love, and men use love in order to get sex.

This has, of course, proven to be a gross simplification of the inter-relationship between sex and emotions for both genders. Nevertheless, clinical experience and sex research has shown that there are differences in the expression, meaning, and experience of sexual and emotional needs for men and women in a relationship.

In general, a woman's sex drive is more affected than a man's is by what is happening in the relationship. A typical example of the connection between relationship satisfaction and female sexual desire arises from the balancing act some women have to perform with work and family. A woman who works outside the home often resents her partner's lack of involvement in domestic chores and childcare, which often diminishes her level of sexual interest. Her partner may interpret this as her punishing him or trying to manipulate him to get her own way and in turn feel quite resentful of her apparent control of his sexual activity. From the woman's point of view, she can't want sex with someone she perceives as not caring about the demands made on her. She believes that if he cared about her, he would put himself out to deal with the tasks at hand. She perceives his failure to voluntarily assist as selfish and the selfishness further demonstrated by his expectation that she should nevertheless have sex with him.

Similarly, a woman will express disbelief if her partner wants to have sex even when they have just had a disagreement. He may see a disagreement as irrelevant to having sex later in the evening or even as a great way to get over the hostility. In contrast, she finds it difficult to respond to his attempts at initiation as long as there is any lingering tension.

A common point of dispute during marriage and sexual counseling arises when the counselor begins to introduce suggestions of strategies for change. Experience shows that if there are significant relationship problems, it is generally counterproductive, at least from the woman's perspective, to suggest that the couple try to increase sexual frequency before some of the difficulties are resolved. The man, however, may inter-pret this as bias on the counselor's part, because from his point of view, an increase in sexual frequency would improve the emotional climate of the relationship for him.

This isn't to say, of course, that all men can or do override emotional issues to pursue sex, but there is some interesting research to support the notion that men tend to seek sex based on recognition of their own needs for either sexual or emotional release, whereas women seek or avoid sex for a much broader range of reasons, including their perception of their partner's needs, their own needs, and the appropriateness of the situa-tion. Research shows that, compared with men, women are more likely to agree to have sex even when they are not sexually aroused and to engage in sexual activities they don't enjoy and may in fact find unpleasant. For example, manual and oral manipulation of the genitals was found to be a turnoff for the majority of the women studied, yet most still engaged in these activities. This indicates that the motivation to engage in sexual activity (that is, sex drive) is more complex for women.

The Affection/Sex Dilemma

In the same way that women and men tend to approach the issue of rela-tionship and sexual problems from opposite ends, couples can get into another chicken-and-egg dilemma with the connection between affection and sex. Although sex may at times be a means for women to obtain love, many women aren't happy with this tradeoff, and they want to be able to give and receive affection without any sexual overtones. Many women typically express annoyance that a man's idea of affectionate touch is often associated with fondling the breasts or genitals, and they usually interpret this as an invitation for sexual activity. As a result, women with low libido may increasingly avoid other forms of affection as well.

Though men may certainly feel the need for affection, they don't see why affectionate touch should exclude playing with a woman's breasts or touching her genitals. If both partners believe that the woman should enjoy this type of touch, her irritation can be taken to confirm the belief that she has serious problems. Yet because it is such a common complaint from women, it seems unlikely that it typically reflects underlying emotional issues. Is there another explanation?

The Influence of Mood

Hormone fluctuations throughout the menstrual cycle can affect levels of physical sex drive for some women, but mood seems to affect almost all women. Although I have talked to some women who feel that their sexual needs are unaffected by tiredness or stress, in general, women tend to find their interest in sex is easily upset by even mild fluctuations in mood and general feelings of well-being. Male sex drive, in contrast, seems much more robust and remains more constant despite normal mood changes.

This difference is reflected in the time it takes to reach orgasm. When a woman is tired, anxious, upset, depressed, or preoccupied, her time to reach orgasm increases; she has to really work hard to get anywhere close to climax. The concept of "working hard" to have an orgasm is quite foreign to most men, who under the same conditions of stress are likely to ejaculate more rapidly than is usual for them. (The condition of inhibited ejaculation during intercourse that some men experience most commonly arises either from a long established pattern of ejaculation to particular masturbatory stimulation or from the effect of drugs, including alcohol.) As sex researcher Dr. John Bancroft has noted, this difference is compelling evidence of biological differences between the sexes: For women, the challenge is to lose control, while for men, it is to gain or keep control.

In addition, many women link their lack of interest in sex to a dislike of being touched and fondled. They point to this as proof of their frigidity without understanding that it is actually more likely to reflect their female sexuality. Not only do women find arousal difficult when they are stressed or tired, attempts at arousal by touch on the breasts or genitals can be quite unpleasant. Stressed men seem to find genital stimulation pleasant and soothing, even if not arousing.

Despite this, breast and genital stimulation are the aspects of foreplay that are regarded as essential. Indeed, many men announce their own desire for sex by touching their partner in these areas. When a woman responds with annoyance and tells her partner to leave her alone, he ends up feeling hurt, and she feels guilty and inadequate.

This difference explains the affection/sex dilemma we discussed previously. If the man touches the woman's breasts or genitals as a way of expressing affection, and she is preoccupied or hassled, she may feel extremely irritated. She may be busy, undressing to change clothes, or just stepping out of the shower when he touches her breast or grabs her between the legs. She is not being cranky, frigid, unreasonable, or unloving in not wanting this type of touch, yet he often interprets it this way, and she lacks the confidence to make him understand her point of view. Over months and years of this happening, she loses enjoyment of touch of any kind, which obviously affects her desire for sex. This may lead to accusations by her partner that she is cold and hard. The injustice of this claim may hurt the woman deeply, but she may also believe there is something wrong with her, so her self-esteem plummets. This sequence of events often leads to increasing emotional distance between the partners.

There is some interesting research on the hormone oxytocin that may help explain a woman's need to be relaxed and happy in order to experience intimate touch as pleasurable. This hormone was first identified for its role in birth and lactation and has been shown in animal studies to make females more sexually receptive. More recent studies show that oxytocin levels in humans increase during touching, cuddling, and other stages of sexual activity. A 1999 study found that oxytocin levels tend to be higher in women who are in a more secure relationship, although there was quite a range of individual differences. It seems likely that for a woman who is tired or hassled, gentle touch, particularly in a good relationship, helps stimulate the flow of oxytocin and thus make her more receptive to sexual activity. Interestingly, oxytocin is produced by both men and women, but for men, the effects are muted by testosterone.

The Importance of Orgasm

The fact that female sex drive and the ability to have orgasms are influenced by both hormonal changes and mood means that at times, arousal and orgasm can be hard work. This has a very important impact on what makes sex good for women. It seems so obvious, yet it is a source of disagreement and discontent for many couples in which the woman is avoiding sex.

Women do not need to experience orgasm with every sexual encounter in order to enjoy it; what's more, if she is stressed or tired, trying hard to have an orgasm can actually make sex *less* enjoyable, even if she does climax. This may be linked to the earlier observation that women don't need to have an orgasm in order to achieve a pregnancy, as well as to the fact that at various times in history, women's role in many societies has been to submit to sex, and whether they achieve orgasm has not been regarded as important. It seems likely that over the course of the evolutionary process, these factors have produced women with a wide variety of orgasmic abilities. Despite the fact that perhaps 10 percent of women never or rarely have an orgasm, they can still have children, meaning that their low orgasmic ability can be passed on to future generations. In contrast, because orgasm usually occurs with ejaculation, men who do not achieve orgasm will not produce offspring to pass on their genes.

Many women who tell me they are frigid back up their belief by saying that they sometimes/often can't have an orgasm. When I ask them whether they might prefer to have sex quietly, without attempts at orgasm, at least some of the time, *most* women nod their heads emphatically!

Because ejaculation and orgasm are integral parts of sexual activity for men, they can find this concept hard to understand. Some men believe they are letting their partner down if she doesn't climax, while other men insist that they don't enjoy sex as much if their partner doesn't become aroused and reach orgasm, so they persist in stimulation no matter how irritating it becomes for the woman or what she says she wants.

This focus on orgasm can have an impact on a woman's interest in sex; after all, a sensible person wants to avoid an annoying or irritating activity! This gives us a clue to the problem of low sex drive: Sex as it is currently idealized does not meet the needs of a lot of women. Resolving this issue is an integral part of making sex an enjoyable activity that they look forward to participating in.

GENDER DIFFERENCES: SUMMING UP

If we put together all of the issues we have explored in this chapter, the picture that emerges is that a woman's sex drive is likely to differ significantly from a man's, particularly from the stereotype of hot, lusty sex drive that dominates in our culture.

Although evolutionary psychological theory is controversial, the conclusion that the sexes developed different reasons to seek sex has gained some support from clinical experience and research results. Women are more likely to seek sex for reasons that are not always related to physical sex drive, and they often find some activities that are currently assumed to be arousing not at all enjoyable, or even annoying. A woman's interest in sex is typically reduced if there is tension or conflict in the relationship.

A common problem for women is difficulty achieving orgasm, and they may in fact enjoy sex more when there is no pressure to even try to climax. As a result, women's experience of sex is often different from men's. Sometimes, emotional satisfaction may be more important than sexual satisfaction.

It's important to reiterate that I am not talking here about the experience of all men or women. There is no doubt that there is tremendous variation among groups of both women and men, so what one woman desires and enjoys can seem quite foreign to another woman. There is also significant overlap between men and women, so some women are more hotly interested in sex and enjoy its physicality more than some men do. It is a bit like differences in height and weight: There is no doubt that gender influences height and weight, and on average, women are shorter and lighter than men, but there are definitely some women who are taller and/or heavier than some men.

Nevertheless, in my clinical experience, the problems some women experience with lack of sexual desire and/or enjoyment are different from those experienced by men.

This has led some authors, such as sexologist Leonore Tiefer, Ph.D., and Dr. Rosemary Basson to challenge the current classification of sexual problems. These authors question the accepted protocol for the diagnosis of sexual dysfunction that is based exclusively on genital performance during heterosexual intercourse. Dr. Tiefer wonders why problems such as "too little tenderness" or "partner has no sense of romance" are not included in the analysis and diagnosis of female sexual problems. This is an exceptionally good question and one that we are now going to address in the next chapter.

CHAPTER 5

IF YOU LOVE ME . . .

RECENTLY IN OUR SOCIETY, THE DEFINITION OF NORMAL SEXUAL FUNCTIONING has shifted emphasis from controlled expression of sexual feelings within strict moral guidelines to uninhibited erotic behavior whenever it seems like a good idea. Not surprisingly, this has caused significant ripples in the traditional connection between love and sex. One of these ripples has changed the accepted idea of the proper sexual expression of love in a marriage. Love has come to equal sexual passion, and lust has been transformed from a sinful state into a virtue in a committed relationship: If you love me, you will lust after me, and if you don't lust after me, how do I know you love me?

Another ripple has caused the reverse connection between sex and love to be abandoned. Sex is no longer to be reserved for a loving relationship. Our society widely accepts casual, recreational sex—pursued and enjoyed for its own sake—independent of any emotional connection between the participants. Popular movies and television shows include casual sex almost routinely, and it's not unusual now for young people to have several sexual partners before establishing a permanent relationship. Yet we still hold onto the belief that a couple in a loving, committed relationship will have a mutually enjoyable sex life characterized by ongoing physical passion that culminates in regular, prolonged erotic encounters.

So what would a man of today expect of his wife, if she loves him? He would hope that she loves him enough to find him physically attractive and desire him. This would mean that she wants to seduce him, and in that seduction, she'll be hot and playful. He would want her to be responsive to his touch, easy to arouse, happy to try different positions and techniques, and able to come to satisfying orgasms, ideally through intercourse. He would expect their sexual encounters to be spontaneous and take place anywhere, not just in the bedroom. He would want her to think about sex as often as he does, to look forward to it when they are apart, and to miss it if too many days pass without it.

What would a woman of today expect of her husband, if he loves her? She would want him to find her sexually attractive and not mind if she isn't the ideal size and shape. She would expect him to know what gets her interested in sex and turns her on, without her having to tell him. She would expect him to be skilled as a lover so he can take her to heights of ecstasy, preferably lasting long enough and performing intercourse in such a way that she can come to orgasm with penile thrusting. She would want their encounters to happen easily, with no awkwardness, and afterward to lie together, basking in the afterglow of making love.

And what would each partner expect of themselves, if they love each other? Shouldn't it be easy to fulfill the hopes and expectations of someone you love so strongly? It is hardly surprising that loving couples happily anticipate an exciting sex life, given that this ideal is heavily promoted by sex and relationship experts. The general theme of sex therapists is that once a couple works through their program for resolving relationship difficulties, their marriage will be erotic and passionate. Obviously, it's logical to worry that if your sex life falls short of this ideal, maybe there is something wrong with your relationship.

Now, I don't doubt that therapies based on these types of programs help some couples achieve the hoped-for result, but I sincerely doubt that they can and do help all couples who wonder about the lack of passion and eroticism in their sex life. The problem may not lie in the process these experts are advocating but rather in the expected outcome. If we acknowledge that there are significant individual and gender differences in the expression of sexuality, might it not also be true that there can be significant differences in the sexual expressions of love, both for a particular couple at different times and for different couples?

LOVE AND SEXUAL BEHAVIOR

Putting aside seemingly self-evident truths and challenging some cherished beliefs can be difficult. When you look at the issue clearly, however, where is the evidence that true love should inevitably lead to a sexually passionate marriage? Imagine partners who are doing everything "right" in their relationship. They treat each other in a caring and generous way, they resolve disagreements respectfully, they spend quality time together, they laugh and cry together, and they share the responsibilities of family and home. Even in this ideal atmosphere, is it absolutely certain that this perfect love will be expressed in an intense and erotic sex life?

To answer this question, we have to return to the nature/nurture debate, particularly the role of culture in shaping the meaning of nonverbal communication. Although there is some consistency in the nonverbal expression of emotions across different cultures, there is also tremendous variety, and a surprising number of behaviors acquire meanings specific to different societies. For example, in some countries, lovers greet each other with restraint, but in Western culture, it is becoming increasingly common for lovers to greet in public with passionate kissing and perhaps even fondling of the buttocks.

If the emotional meaning attached to specific behaviors can be determined by the forces of society, is it possible that the accepted manner in which love between a man and a woman is expressed sexually can also be shaped by prevailing cultural values?

In my own lifetime, I have seen such changes occur. As discussed earlier, typical advice for women in the 1950s and 1960s was that they should not be too forward sexually. When I began to practice as a sex therapist in the 1970s, I saw couples in which the man complained that his wife was being too aggressive because she would often initiate sex. Rather than seeing their wife's advances as expressions of love, some men felt intimidated by them. (For example, one man I saw was unable to get an erection if his wife initiated sex.)

Similarly, even now, I see women who are highly offended by their partner's attempts to stimulate them orally, saying that they feel this cheapens their love and makes them feel like prostitutes. Some women feel disgusted when they find out that their partners masturbate or even look at other women, believing that this behavior is disrespectful and demonstrates a lack of love for them.

What does this mean about the belief and the hope that if you work through any relationship issues and feel secure in your love for each other, you should be able to achieve an erotic, passionate marriage? It means that it certainly can't be guaranteed. The relationship between love and specific sexual behaviors, such as feeling physical passion and wanting to initiate sex with your beloved, is not an ingrained human behavior that is set for all human beings. Rather, it's currently the preferred behavior in our society.

This is not to deny that for some people, the connection between love and raunchy sex does exist. There are many couples who will happily attest that for them it does, at least some of the time. But even if all of society were to agree that the best way to express deep love in a relationship is with lusty, varied, spontaneous sexual behavior, could everybody do it?

Here we come back to the importance of individual and gender differences. No matter how much we may wish it to be so, even if two partners are equal in their commitment and love for each other, they will usually differ in the many ways in which that love translates to their sexual relationship.

EMOTIONS:
THE FORGOTTEN SUBTEXT OF SEX

Believing that love is expressed only through passionate sex has resulted in a more impoverished emotional life. As we become more focused on doing it right, sex seems to have been reduced to a series of behaviors for which the main concern is, Did you come? rather than, Did you feel loved? We talk about "making love," but many of the couples I see tell me that it usually feels like they are "having sex," which they describe as lacking emotional intimacy.

What words are commonly used to describe the current ideal of great sex? The list would include *sizzling, passionate, erotic, hot, lusty, raunchy, exciting, fiery, intense,* and *ecstatic,* as well as *loving* and maybe *tender.* Words that are unlikely to be used are *comforting, accepting, gentle, patient, still, quiet, reassuring, peaceful, pleasant, simple, kind,* and *soothing.* Now this isn't a competition to find the best—or most correct—words. There's no doubt that if a couple can have sizzling, intense, hot sex, they are onto a good thing that they should cherish. However, the absence of the more deeply emotional words in our sexual vocabulary suggests that the current understanding of the role of sex in a long-term relationship is somewhat limited and that far from opening up the sexual potential of a couple, it's closing it down. We have thought of the last 50 years as ushering in the sexual revolution and offering sexual liberation to couples, but in fact we merely exchanged one set of rules that undermine our sexual freedom for another.

The focus on practicing the "right" behaviors to express love can undermine a healthy relationship in two ways. If those behaviors don't occur—if the couple's sex life falls far short of the current stereotype of great sex—the quality of their love and the strength of their commitment can be called into question. Thus, if the woman doesn't initiate sex, surely that must mean that she doesn't love her partner, at least not enough or not in a normal way, or maybe she doesn't find him attractive.

If the couple *can* have the accepted "great sex," or the woman is hotly seductive some of the time, this can lead to the belief that this is the way it should be all the time. If not, one or both partners are being selfish or missing out, and that can't be right if they care about each other. This pressure to get it right on every occasion can lead to performance anxiety, less enjoyment, and, in time, avoidance of sex.

In this sexualized society, we like to believe that we are very flexible in what we expect in a good sex life, and this generally includes accepting variety in terms of sexual techniques, such as oral sex or sex games. Previous generations are regarded as having been inflexible because of their conservative views about normal sexual behavior. However, inflexibility in expecting erotic and passionate sex to be the only genuine expression of an emotionally healthy relationship is just as restrictive and damaging.

If a couple has deep and committed love for each other, the emotional subtext of sex can be scrambled if they rely on only one form of sex to express that love. If sex is thought to communicate messages of love and caring, and if the "right" behaviors don't occur, how do the partners interpret what is happening? I see many couples in good relationships who experience this: They are confused because they feel that their emotional relationship is fine, yet their sex life seems off-kilter. What does this mean? Does she love me? Can I really love him if I don't feel like having sex with him? Am I being a selfish lover if I don't make the effort to bring her to orgasm, no matter how long it takes? Am I being unfair if I don't give him oral sex even though I don't like it? Is she unhappy in our relationship if she pushes me away when I try to cuddle and caress her during the day? How can I love him when his touch often annoys me?

It's obvious that in a long-term relationship, the emotional messages that are given and received strengthen or undermine the relationship. Some messages are clear, such as when the partners can tell each other about their feelings, but some messages are sent by the way they behave together. Sex is an important arena for intimate communication, even if few words are spoken. If the tie between emotions and sexual behaviors is flawed, a potentially sound relationship can falter. Doubts about the meaning of what is happening in their sex life, and the lack of confidence to express feelings of love and caring in ways that are appropriate and meaningful to the couple, mean that the couple's sense of security in the marriage can be severely limited.

Although this emotional world is not the exclusive domain of women, the absence of emotional as opposed to physical intimacy seems to distress women more than it does men. In seeking to answer the questions, What is sex drive? and What is good sex? failure to recognize the need for reassurance, comfort, and emotional connection as important aspects of sex leaves the sexual relationship barren for many women.

RELATIONSHIP SEX

There is a simple answer to this dilemma. It involves seeing through the sexual illusion to what might be possible and meaningful for each couple. If we abandon the notion that sex is about what is done and replace it with the idea that sex is about the whole range of emotions that bind the couple as a unit, satisfying sex can be within easy reach. In a sense, a couple can't fail at sex if they have a sound, caring relationship characterized by mutual goodwill. Whatever they can do on any particular occasion, given who they are and what is happening in their lives at that time, becomes what is right, even if it is a little disappointing on the hot-and-happening scale. I call this type of sex *relationship sex*. In my experience, some couples have already worked this out for themselves and are enjoying contented, hassle-free sex lives, but there are others who lack the confidence to accept what's quite obvious.

The idea of relationship sex is based on the assumption that the probability of a person having serious sexual dysfunction is actually quite low. It also assumes that the primary function of sex in a long-term relationship is to enhance the couple's emotional connection and that this is not dependent on specific behaviors, such as who initiates sex or what techniques the couple prefers. Once the range of individual and gender differences is taken into account, there is enormous diversity in human sexuality, and the range of options open to the couple to determine what constitutes an enjoyable, meaningful, and satisfying sexual relationship is correspondingly large. By starting with the assumption that the two individuals in the relationship are likely to be perfectly normal, the couple's task is to find out over time what works for them. In this process, they accept that sex does not remain unaffected by the ebb and flow of daily life.

There seems to be a common expectation that sex should take place within a magic bubble that somehow shields it from the day-to-day stresses most people experience. Sometimes there is acceptance that maybe sex isn't so good on a particular day because of an unusual amount of stress, but generally, we are unprepared for the reality that ordinary life can limit sex for days, weeks, months, and maybe even years at a time, with perhaps brief flashes of passion and fire from time to time.

Many men say that they believe their partner is just making excuses about being tired or hassled in order to avoid having sex. I find this an extraordinary concept, because I'm not really clear about what is meant. Is the woman using the fact that she is tired to avoid sex? In other words, does she really not want sex? Well, of course! There seems to be an implication that this means there is a dark and mysterious reason behind her need to use fatigue as an "excuse" instead of acceptance of the facts— she's tired, she doesn't want sex—and realization that there is a reasonable connection between these two points. If this is the situation, the question then becomes whether there's some way to make sex a pleasant option for her even though she is tired and uptight.

Relationship sex also recognizes that a person's mood varies from happy to sad, optimistic to worried, lively to flat, and so on, and the emotional connection between the partners can also shift. These varying emotional states will inevitably be played out in the sexual arena. Although negative emotions quite reasonably can lead to outright unwillingness to have sex, sometimes sex can be an opportunity to tentatively reestablish connection (although in this case, sexual expression would be more restrained). But there are many emotions that can all be expressed in the sexual relationship that would change the way the couple has sex. Think about expressing tenderness, compassion, sadness, concern, or just "Hi, isn't it good we've made it through another day?" This emotion-driven sex is likely to be quite different from that driven by physical passion.

The final and possibly most significant aspect of relationship sex is the recognition of the importance of individual and gender differences in sexuality. Each person has a particular sexual language: that is, the emotions a person brings to sex, the way he expresses these emotions, and the style in which he pursues physical desires and needs. The task of the couple is to learn to interpret and appreciate each other's language. This is not a mystical process but plain common sense. If a couple has a solid, loving relationship that suits them, it makes sense to use that as the starting point for building their sexual relationship over time. They may think, If we trust our love and know that we are not out to hurt each other, what we are doing and how we are expressing ourselves sexually must be valid and appropriate for us. In other words, at the present time, we have the cart before the horse. For example, many of us may think, Because she doesn't initiate sex, she must not love her partner. Relationship sex reverses this: Given that she loves her partner, if she doesn't initiate sex, there must be a good reason, and she will have her own way of sexually expressing her love.

When a couple takes this obvious step, self-doubt about how sexually normal they are disappears. There are two people in the relationship; both have their own values about sex, their own desires and needs, and their similarities and differences. Rather than focusing on what might be missing, they explore what is present. Rather than worrying that there must be a lot wrong between them because they are not having ideal sex, they focus on what is right, because they know their choice to share their lives is a good one. Rather than being hurt that there are some things they may never experience sexually, they experience good-natured disappointment.

Humor plays an important role in relationship sex. When things don't go according to plan, instead of feeling let down and distressed, it's freeing to see the funny side. Say you tried to shift from one position to another, and you literally came apart at the seams. Or your partner got a cramp while using manual stimulation to bring you to orgasm. Or your jaw suddenly locked as you were performing oral sex. Which reaction reflects sexual maturity: both of you dealing with the situation with a smile and a shrug, then moving on to something else, or becoming anxious and guilty that you've done the wrong thing, which is confirmed when your partner seems annoyed?

Sex manuals advise couples to play sex games to liven up their sex life, and the usual suggestions are things like dressing up in sexy clothing or acting out fantasies. That's fine as far as it goes, but this can become a pressure in itself. In relationship sex, play is more a state of mind, a sense of relaxation together that lets the couple feel lighthearted so that laughter and giggles aren't out of place.

Because there is no behavioral formula for relationship sex, it can be brief and tender, it can be quiet and comforting, it can be slow and sensual. Some couples have particular tried-and-true formulas they rely on because they are familiar, easy, and comforting in times of stress. Other couples have sex that ranges from 5-minute sessions that meet the needs of the moment to prolonged encounters when time and energy permit. At times, each partner will need different things from sex, and one or both may not get what they're looking for, but sometimes that's just the way it is. The aim is to achieve a good enough balance over time so that on some occasions, the less energetic person nevertheless makes an effort to do more for her partner, and at other times, the one who is more keen accepts getting less than he had hoped for with good grace. Any couple can have a great sex life when they are always evenly matched and want the same style of sex; it's when they experience difficult times that the depth and strength of their relationship is revealed.

Breaking All the Rules

Relationship sex works on the principle that the couple needs to abandon many of the rules that seem to have developed in recent years about what should happen in a sexual relationship and instead develop their sex life to suit themselves. Yet these arbitrary rules can be difficult

GOOD SEX

Although this example may not make it as a scene in an erotic movie or romance novel, in my view it reflects a sexual relationship that is as meaningful and satisfying as any that is always easily passionate and erotic.

The young mother was exhausted, and she fell gratefully into bed. After a while, she felt her husband move toward her and pull her gently into a cuddle. She realized it had been more than a week since they had had sex, and her first thought was a tired, "I can't be bothered." They lay in each other's arms for a while, talking quietly about their day, fearful of waking the child sleeping in the next room. He stroked her face, then tickled her arms lightly. She relaxed against him and moved her hands across his chest. She felt him tentatively touch her breasts, an expression of hope that she might be ready to respond as she used to. She laughed and said with genuine regret, "It would be nice, wouldn't it?" as she moved away from him and took the lubricant from the bedside table. After she had used it, she lay back down and pulled him toward her. She could see his face in the half light, and she touched it tenderly. He murmured that he loved her, then carefully entered her. She sighed and enjoyed the feel of his skin against hers. She was asleep before he finished. He lay back and rested a moment before he reached over and carefully pulled the covers over her, then he too fell into a welcome sleep.

to recognize because they have blended so completely into the accepted sexual picture. I have chosen six rules that seem very influential at this time, but there are likely to be others. However, these rules sufficiently illustrate the value of challenging anything we believe "should" happen in a sexual relationship.

A couple should have sex frequently and regularly. The obvious point to raise, of course, is what is meant by "frequent and regular." Some people believe that sex should happen daily, others believe that normal couples have sex at least a couple of times a week, and some accept that once a week is reasonable. However, couples who have sex only once a month, or even less often, are usually thought to have a problem.

One woman was referred to me by her doctor, who was concerned when the woman decided to change her form of contraception from the Pill to a diaphragm. She told her doctor that she thought the Pill was overkill because she and her husband had sex only a couple of times a year. Convinced that this must indicate sexual dysfunction, the doctor made the referral to me. I saw the woman on her own, then her husband by himself, and then the couple together. The result of these consultations was that both partners agreed that they were quite happy with the way things were; neither was particularly interested in sex, but both enjoyed it when it happened.

Whether a couple isn't inclined to have sex with any definite pattern, or whether life stresses mean that sexual frequency fluctuates, relationship sex adapts to their circumstances at any given time in their lives.

A good sexual session should last at least half an hour. It can be somewhat intimidating to hear some couples talk of lost weekends during which they rarely leave the bed, surfacing only to get food and drink. Although this may be the gold standard that we fantasize about, it's difficult to fit it into a busy life, when trying to find even a half hour on a regular basis can be problematic.

Some couples know each other so well that they just don't need more than 15 minutes from beginning to end for them both to be satisfied.

Although magazine articles urge readers not to let their sex lives get dull and boring, this represents a huge assumption that more time and activity mean less boredom and more enjoyment. Why mess with a formula that is keeping both parties happy?

There are also times when partners are already really keen for sex and don't need much foreplay. Perhaps they have been watching a sexy movie, or they haven't had an opportunity to have sex for a while, or they are just delighted to see each other. Whatever the reason, if they are already highly aroused, they may just want to get their clothes off and get straight to it.

Quite commonly, sexual sessions are brief simply because one or both partners can't be bothered with a longer effort. It may be late, there may be an early start in the morning, or there may be just no energy to try to set the world on fire. To extend foreplay under these circumstances can be extremely irritating. A quiet, brief session satisfies the need for an easy orgasm or a quiet cuddle. This is essentially the "Hi, how are you?" sex that helps couples stay in touch.

Each partner should know what the other wants. I have never seen movie sex scenes where the couple actually communicates about what they want or what is or isn't working. The media message is that good lovers know how to please each other and that good sex is a harmonious blending of united souls who flow easily along the path to ecstasy.

Unfortunately, sexual needs and desires change from day to day, and few people are mind readers. This doesn't mean that a couple needs a 10-minute planning session before every sexual encounter, but "that's nice" or "not here, there" or moving a hand or mouth where it's wanted isn't a sign that you are an inadequate lover.

It doesn't matter whether a couple has been together for 10 days, 10 months, or 10 years—communication is an essential part of relationship sex. Over time, a couple may read each other's cues more clearly so that communication is more subtle—a slight sigh, a touch on the bottom, and so on. Sometimes, though, the message has to be clear: "I've switched off, let's move on" or a definite body movement to get things moving more quickly. This isn't criticism of the partner's ability as a lover, yet some couples I talk with believe there should be no need to communicate during sex. I hear comments such as "Shouldn't he know what I want?" and "If she is telling me what she wants, does she think I don't know how to be a good lover?"

Of course, the other side of communication is listening. There isn't much point in speaking up if what you say is ignored. Usually, one partner ignores what the other is saying if it doesn't fit with what he wants to hear. This is a major issue for women who repeatedly tell their partner that they can't just flick a switch and turn on instantly, that what happens outside the bedroom makes a difference in how interested they are in sex, and that they need a soft touch before they start getting too serious. When this information is disregarded, the woman is likely to eventually give up on sex.

Unfortunately, many couples who do communicate do so only in the negative: "Leave me alone," "Don't do that," or "I don't like this." This gives your partner absolutely no idea what would please you. Learning to say what you *would* like, positively and confidently, makes it easier for your partner to listen.

Sex should never be awkward or clumsy. The same movies that never show a couple communicating also leave out the bits where sex doesn't go according to plan. You never see a couple having difficulty with penetration, needing two or three attempts and maybe some assistance from the woman before the penis goes in easily. You never see a couple fall apart when they try to shift positions, or one partner accidentally poking the other in the eye, although hopefully these incidents are relatively infrequent. You certainly never see the woman having difficulty coming to orgasm as her partner patiently stimulates her clitoris with his hand, his mind starting to wander and his erection waning. If oral sex is simulated in erotic movies, the woman never gags, and the man's jaw never starts to lock. Although it's common for a woman to bring her partner to orgasm with manual stimulation, particularly if she isn't as interested in sex and does this as an alternative, this is rarely shown in movies, and nobody ever talks about the fact that if he takes a while to come, her shoulder and back can start to ache, and her hand gets very tired.

All of these situations are perfectly normal, yet couples are often embarrassed to talk about them, worrying that it means they don't do sex very well or fearing that any comments are meant as criticism. Certainly, some people don't cope when things aren't ideal. One man who came to see me got annoyed with his wife when she had a leg cramp during intercourse and wanted to stop, saying to her angrily, "How can you think of that at a time like this?!" And a woman can be quite critical if her partner doesn't last as long as she thinks he should or loses his erection during foreplay that's focused on arousing her.

Generally, though, the people I talk with worry more that their own performance will let their partner down rather than being concerned about the partner's performance.

Relationship sex assumes that people are doing the best they can, so all of these mishaps are to be expected at least once in a while— sometimes frustrating, sometimes amusing, but not catastrophes.

Saying no to your partner is wrong. I have said several times that I don't believe we have progressed very far toward sexual enlightenment but have merely traded one set of rigid stereotypes for another. Traditionally, sex in marriage was seen as a sacred duty to be performed for the procreation of the species, whether or not it was enjoyable for one or both partners. Usually, this meant that the wife was supposed to submit herself to her husband's advances. The women's movement challenged this belief, and the sex-for-pleasure movement reinforced the idea that the aim of sex is to make it a mutually enjoyable experience. It seems obvious to me that if one partner absolutely does not feel like having sex, it shouldn't occur. Imagine my surprise, then, to find sex therapists advocating the "sex is supreme" approach.

Ruth Westheimer, Ph.D., for example, in a 1992 *Ask Dr. Ruth* column, admonished one woman who found her libido reduced following childbirth that she was going to have big problems in her marriage if she didn't change her attitude. Dr. Ruth advised that she shouldn't tell her partner she didn't feel like having sex but should satisfy him one way or another whenever he wanted, even if that was every day. Yet another example of a sex therapist pressuring people into believing that they don't have any rights in their sexual relationship if they don't conform to the great sex stereotype.

I have seen couples who have been to other therapists who have similarly advised that the partner with the lower sex drive should give the other person sex whenever he or she wants it.

This advice, that sexual wants or needs are more important than any other aspect of a relationship, is reflected in comments by my clients who feel that their partner is being entirely unreasonable in not giving in to sex; after all, said one man, "we've all got to do things we don't particularly want to do."

To me, there seem to be so many grounds to challenge this belief that I hardly know where to start. It's one thing to feel that you are not particularly interested in sex for yourself but to be quite willing and happy to sometimes have sex with your partner simply because it's reassuring to you both in some way. However, to feel that you *must* have sex, or that you are obligated to perform a sexual activity of any kind to give your partner release, seems to me to be a recipe for disaster. Unwanted sex over an extended period is highly likely to lead to annoyance, resentment, and sadness, which will make sex less desirable and lessen any chance that the low-drive person's desire will increase.

I understand that not having your sexual needs met can also lead to feelings of rejection and resentment, but how helpful is it to badger your partner into sex? Although it may sometimes lead to your partner giving in, it's also likely to lead to feelings of resentment or anger. After all, don't most people feel annoyed when they are pressured into doing something they really don't want to do?

In my view, the best chance for a couple to develop a mutually enjoyable sex life and relationship generally is to recognize that sex can be a positive experience only when there is something in it for both partners. For this to happen, you have to be able to confidently say no to sex when it isn't okay and to happily say yes when it is.

Sex should always be enjoyable. In a relationship that has spanned years or decades, it's inevitable that at least on some occasions, a sexual session will be a complete disaster. More than being just dull, it may be uncomfortable, irritating, or annoying, and you may be left feeling angry, disappointed, or resentful. If this happens infrequently, it's usually just part of what's normal over time. Most couples are realistic and develop their own ways of dealing with it. They may be unhappy for a day or two, but they can put it into perspective and not interpret it as a symptom of sexual dysfunction or allow it to threaten the stability of their caring relationship. These experiences allow the care and concern the couple have for each other to eventually resolve any tensions, and most couples are philosophical enough to let such incidents pass.

Listen to Your Own Needs

Whenever you feel worried about any aspect of your sex life, don't automatically assume that you are the problem. Try to identify what you believe you *should* be doing, and ask yourself, How did I come to feel this way? Where is the evidence that things should be that way? Why is it a problem if I do things differently? What does my partner want? (Often, it's a relief to talk the issue through and realize that it isn't as important to him as you had thought.) The only rule worth sticking to is to ignore any rule that makes sex become a hassle.

THINKING OUTSIDE THE BOX

It's not my intention to replace one prescription for good sex with another. Relationship sex is not and cannot be the same thing to all couples.

Many years ago, a middle-aged woman came to see me because sex had become painful. She hadn't told her husband and continued to endure their weekly sexual encounters in silence. The problem was easily identified: Not only was she menopausal and suffering from a dry vagina, but she had used petroleum jelly for many years as a sexual lubricant because she never became aroused and wet. Petroleum jelly was a popular lubricant for many couples before better-quality products became available, but it can have the side effect of irritating the vagina, thus creating a continuing need for a lubricant.

At the time, I was a young therapist and a keen advocate of sexual pleasure for women, so I began to talk with her about the importance of discussing with her husband how she felt and perhaps exploring ways of making sex more enjoyable for her. The woman's reaction to this was a major learning experience for me. She made it clear that my interest and suggestions were unwelcome—all she wanted was advice on how to stop the pain so she could be more comfortable doing her marital duty. I realized that despite what I felt about how this couple was conducting their sex life, it was what felt right and meaningful to the woman, and I obviously had no right to interfere.

The idea of relationship sex is to encourage couples to think outside the current beliefs about the love/sex connection and the focus on only one type of sexual relationship, and discover what works for them. Every assumption about "If you love me. . ." needs to be recognized, challenged, and abandoned if it's causing doubt and distress. Some couples may find early on that their loving sexual relationship is at odds with the passionate and erotic concept of good sex, and others may have to deal with that only when they hit a time in their lives when they are unable to sustain their usual energy and enthusiasm for sex.

In general, I believe that it takes time for most couples to develop their own easygoing, hassle-free sex lives. In this age of instant gratification, taking time to develop a good sex life seems absurd. Many people think that they should be able to get into bed and have everything just work, even if they are a little anxious. But many of the older couples I have talked with, who consulted me because of some difficulties associated with aging, say that when they got married, they expected it to take months or even years to develop a harmonious sexual relationship that was enjoyable to both.

A lot of people I see aren't worried for themselves but feel that they're letting their partner down in some way because their sex life isn't following the ideal script. It can be incredibly liberating for many long-term couples to realize that what they are already doing is actually right for them. Unfortunately, many couples are bewildered and often in great distress about what is happening in their sex life. They are often caught in a cycle of unrealistic expectations and misunderstandings, so that what began as a simple case of mismatched libidos can escalate into catastrophes for their relationship.

CHAPTER 6

WHEN WANTS AND NEEDS DON'T MATCH

DURING MY 30 YEARS AS A SEX THERAPIST, I have talked with hundreds of women and their partners who were worried about the woman's low libido. Most of these couples are reasonable people in essentially sound relationships and living everyday lives. Usually, they are both doing the best they can, trying to treat each other with concern and respect. So how do these caring and sensible people end up feeling so distressed in their sexual relationship?

Although low libido is often assumed to be the result of some kind of physical or psychological pathology, the core issues of unrealistic sexual expectations, lack of appreciation of individual differences, and misunderstandings about male and female sexuality account for more than half of the cases I see, with no other, more serious contributing factors. These expectations and misunderstandings trigger a cycle of confusion and worry that eventually erodes a couple's sexual self-confidence and wears down any interest in sex the woman may have. Here's how the cycle works.

THE ANTI-LIBIDO CYCLE

Most couples in the early stages of their relationship believe they have achieved, or have the potential to achieve, a mutually satisfying sex life.

The strong emotions of attraction and infatuation usually make it easy to want to be close, to touch, and to be sexually intimate. Over time, the intensity of these feelings tends to wane, and once the couple begins to live together, the cues that help a woman become interested in sex occur less frequently. When a couple is dating, they focus on each other, spend time together, talk intimately, caress gently—and these things help develop her sexual desire. As the couple develops a daily routine, many of these cues decrease. The partners both work, come home, chat briefly, prepare dinner, clean up, do the chores, and fall into bed, and the first sense of intimacy the woman may get is when her partner tries to initiate sex by exploring her body. If she's tired, this does little for her, and she would prefer not to bother. Passion has given way to practical matters.

There are couples who understand this and accept the decrease in intensity of sexual feelings as reasonable, and they adjust their sex life accordingly. They make sure, however, that they do get time to relax and connect emotionally on a regular basis, and they work out what they need to do between them to maintain regular and enjoyable sex.

Unfortunately, it doesn't work out that way for all couples. Sometimes quite early in the relationship—and sometimes not for many years—the differences in needs and wants begin to create tension. At this stage, the couple should acknowledge that their differences are a result of mismatched libidos rather than thinking one or the other is dysfunctional. By doing so, they could tackle their problems without hurt or blame. Instead, however, many couples find themselves caught up in an ever-deepening cycle of increasing tension and emotional hurt that magnifies the differences between them. The following factors all contribute to the cycle.

Expectations

For most women who ultimately come to believe that they have problems with their libido, the spiral downward from being confident or at least optimistic about their sexuality to a conviction that they are sexually inadequate begins when they first experience a sense of reluctance in response to their partner's attempts to initiate sex. This reluctance may surface in the early stages of a relationship, when a couple is dating and the woman realizes that it's assumed that sex will happen whenever they get together, or perhaps it arises after many years of enthusiasm for sex, when a period of stress occurs. The defining moment is when she feels that she's expected (by herself and/or her partner) to desire sex and instead feels only tiredness or irritation, and she wonders if something is wrong. It may be that the first few times this happens, she and her partner pass it off as temporary, but when it persists, concern grows.

There are other expectations that put pressure on a woman and affect her interest in sex. The first of these, as we have seen, relates to what sexual desire is supposed to be. When she realizes that she rarely feels the level of lustfulness that her friends talk about or that she sees portrayed in the movies, she starts to wonder if there is something wrong with her. Why doesn't she experience the overwhelming physical need for sex that she has been led to expect? Perhaps she becomes worried when her partner comments at some stage that she never seems to be the one to initiate sex.

Of course, if her partner expects sex more often than she does, the woman may believe she has low libido even if she wants sex weekly or more often. On the other hand, if she and her partner share similar ideas about reasonable and normal sexual frequency (whether it's once a day or once a month), her particular level of sex drive is unlikely to be a problem.

Even well-matched partners are likely to find that there are times when one feels like having sex and the other doesn't. If, subtly or blatantly, a woman's partner conveys to her that he would like sex and expects it will happen, without determining how she feels about it, she may feel annoyed by what she perceives as his lack of consideration for her. If this happens often enough, she can start to believe that he is more interested in her body than in her as a person, dampening her sexual desire. Eventually, just knowing he wants or expects sex can be enough to turn her off, no matter how considerate he tries to be. Often, this completely misrepresents the man's feelings and intentions, but the couple has become caught in a no-win situation in which he can't initiate sex when he feels like it, and she doesn't initiate sex because she never feels like it, so frequency inevitably declines.

The other situation in which a sense of expectation may lessen a woman's desire is when there is disagreement about what should happen during sex. Whatever the woman's motivation for sex, she may frequently avoid it if the expectation is that she should engage in activities she doesn't usually enjoy, that don't suit her current mood, or that continue for longer than she feels she can sustain with any level of pleasure. If the man is more focused on experimentation, activity, arousal, and orgasm, and the woman prefers relatively brief, quiet, passive, sensual lovemaking, she will lack the enthusiasm to respond to his desire. Because society endorses the view that sex should be busy and passionate, the woman often feels powerless to make her needs be heard and understood. Over time, if she feels her partner's preferred sexual activity is irritating, annoying, hard work, or uncomfortable, her reluctance to have sex will grow.

Thirty years ago, however, the situation was quite different. At that time, the problem was more likely to be insufficient time spent on foreplay, so women rarely had the opportunity to experience any degree of arousal, and they wondered what was wrong with them. Then, the plea would have been for longer foreplay. Now that the common expectation seems to be that sex must include intense stimulation of the breasts or clitoris in the relentless pursuit of orgasm, some women quietly envy their predecessors!

A woman may also have unreasonable expectations in that she may have fallen for the belief that if her partner loves her and is a considerate lover, he will know what she needs and enjoys without her having to tell him. She may also expect that his touch should produce "rivers of fire" in her body, as she has read in romance novels, and believe he is a poor lover when this doesn't happen.

Initiation

Often, the way a man goes about trying to get his partner interested in sex means he is destined to fail from the beginning. Certainly, a direct question such as "How about it?" or "Want to make love?" does little to get a woman in the mood. Images from erotic films give the impression that the woman should respond with enthusiasm to direct sexual stimulation, often beginning with passionate kissing and stimulation of the breasts and genitals, without any preliminaries, such as talking, cuddling, or massage. Unfortunately, this is quite off-putting to a woman who has her mind on entirely nonsexual matters at the time. If one or both partners interpret her desire to push him away as a symptom of her problem, they don't explore more appropriate techniques for initiating sex, and it takes effort on the woman's part to overcome her physical irritation and continue with sexual activity. Eventually, she tries to avoid his touch or shrugs him off with annoyance, leaving them both hurt and bewildered.

As we have seen, however, sometimes a man can't win either way: If his partner knows he is expecting sex at the end of it all, even a quiet dinner followed by lots of cuddling and massage may not work.

Sometimes, the man will adopt the strategy of not initiating sex himself, hoping that eventually his partner will experience some sense of sexual tension and approach him. This rarely works. Months may go by without the thought of sex occurring to her! It's difficult for a person who regularly experiences physical desire for sex to understand that in many cases, someone who lacks that desire could live quite happily without sex. The challenge is to find anything at all that might help make sex more attractive to her.

Often, the man expresses hurt and dismay that he is the one who always has to initiate sex. He may interpret this as a personal rejection ("she doesn't find me attractive") or feel that he is missing out on an important part of sex, that is, being seduced by someone who desires him. Unfortunately, at least for the short term, this situation is unlikely to change. It makes sense to focus on developing more appropriate ways for the man to initiate sex and for the couple to accept that he may remain the primary initiator of sex.

The key to the problem of initiation is for the woman to know that she has a choice, both in terms of saying yes or no to sex and in how sex is conducted when she does say yes. This brings us to the next factor operating in the anti-libido cycle.

Reaction

A man's reaction to his partner's early reluctance to have sex and to her definite refusals is critical in the future direction of their sexual relationship. If he is understanding and considerate, even if he's disappointed, it's likely that over time, the couple will come to a give-and-take balance in their sexual relationship. If, however, he becomes sulky, angry, abusive, or withdrawn, the woman clearly gets the message that she is being unreasonable in not meeting his needs.

Sometimes, a negative reaction indicates the man's sense of entitlement in the relationship. Some men (fortunately, a small minority) believe that being in a relationship entitles them to sex whenever and however they want it. Such a man is likely to react with criticism, hostility, and anger if the woman rejects his sexual advances or won't engage in a sexual activity he wants. He will say that he should not be forced to miss out on what he wants and that she is being unreasonable or controlling by withholding sex from him.

Withdrawing, sulking, getting agitated, or crying may indicate that the man is sexually dependent and that he relies on sex to cope with his life generally and to bolster his self-esteem. In my experience, men are more likely to be sexually dependent than women. A sexually dependent person experiences strong, persistent sexual feelings that compel him to seek sexual release. He is often preoccupied with his sexual need and expects to have sex based on that need, with little or no consideration for his partner's feelings, often using emotional manipulation to get his need met. He is, for example, likely to use the argument that if she loves him, she should want to have sex when he does or do what he needs.

Unfortunately, in cases of either entitlement or dependency, it's usually difficult to engage the man in the counseling process because he firmly believes the problem lies with his partner. The most useful strategy to take in therapy is to focus on helping the woman recognize her rights in the relationship and develop the assertiveness to seek them.

It's certainly understandable that a man may feel disappointed that sex doesn't occur when he wants it and to feel concerned if sexual encounters are almost nonexistent. But punitive reactions such as not talking, refusing to share responsibility for household chores, becoming abusive, or, as in the case of one couple I saw, confiscating the keys to the car, are not healthy and helpful ways to solve the problem. Similarly, becoming annoyed or critical because the woman doesn't want to participate in a particular type of sexual activity is hardly likely to help her want and enjoy it.

Sometimes, a woman feels sufficiently intimidated to give in to her partner; she may want to avoid an argument or may feel guilty that she is being unreasonable. Unfortunately, this tends to lead to feelings of resentment and anger during sex, making the experience worse for her and increasing her lack of interest. And so the anti-libido cycle spins a bit faster, as her focus increasingly changes from her own needs to engaging in sex to keep her partner happy or quiet.

The woman's reactions during sex are also significant. How does she react when her partner does something that doesn't please her? Does she become tearful—or scornful? How can her partner learn what is soothing, pleasurable, or arousing if she gives him only such negative reactions? His options for pleasing her become more and more limited as she lets him know what she doesn't like but gives him no clue about what might make sex better for her.

Criticism, conflict, argument, and verbal abuse have no role in a caring, satisfying sexual relationship. The sad thing is that many men really don't want to seem unreasonable and demanding, but they don't know how to deal with their disappointment and sadness about their sexual difficulties. The style of communication the couple uses can make or break their relationship.

Communication

Communication in a relationship is important at several levels. Obviously, a couple who can chat about almost anything, who can solve disagreements respectfully, and who find it easy to let each other know what they like about each other are likely to enjoy being in a relationship together. Good, positive, effective communication in general helps to create an atmosphere that will promote sexual interest in each other.

A great deal is said and written about the importance of sexual communication. Couples who seek help for low libido often acknowledge that they do not communicate well and seem to be at a loss to know what to do about it. Solving communication problems isn't as simple as it sounds. A number of essential elements are often missing when a couple tries to talk about the difficulties they are experiencing.

The first essential is knowledge. If she doesn't know that it's normal for her to have an orgasm only sometimes or only through foreplay rather than intercourse, how can communication solve the problem? If he genuinely believes that unless she is really hot to have sex with him, she doesn't find him attractive, how does he talk to her about his distress? A great deal of sexual communication is based on false, unrealistic expectations, so nothing is resolved.

It's also difficult to communicate effectively without confidence. If the woman believes she is frigid or inadequate, her attempts at communication will be flawed by guilt, apology, and submission. Her needs can't be met because she—and certainly her partner—will never recognize and state them. Only by believing in her own sexuality, and her right to her unique set of likes, dislikes, level of interest, and so on, can she be an equal partner in the communication process.

Obviously, the style of communication is important: It needs to be positive. For example: "This makes it better for me; that's not so good" or "I don't feel like sex, but I'd love a cuddle" rather than the negative "I've told you a hundred times I don't like that" or "For heaven's sake, can't you see I'm tired?" or, worse still (from the man), "What's wrong with you; are you frigid?" and "Well, I didn't have this problem with my other partners."

The final essential of good communication is being prepared to listen and to work out solutions that are good enough for both partners. Communication based on scoring points or focusing on trying to get one partner to give in to the other's point of view is a complete waste of time. There is no point in clear and confident communication about what either partner thinks or feels or wants if it's immediately dismissed, or if no attempt is made to understand the other's perspective.

For one person's point of view to be right, the other's doesn't have to be wrong. I find that most commonly with differences in libido, what each of the partners thinks, feels, and wants is understandable and reasonable. The couple's task is to keep talking and listening with goodwill and respect so that individual points of view are acknowledged and taken into account. It's possible to work through the issues associated with differences in libido when partners can discuss their problems with generosity and concern for each other's well-being. Without clear, positive, confident communication, problems fester, and the anti-libido cycle spins more rapidly.

Misinterpretation

Often, a lot of the damage done by differences in libido is due not to what is actually happening but to how each person interprets the other's behavior.

For the man who is in a relationship with a woman who doesn't seem to want sex with him, he tends to interpret her lack of interest as:

- She doesn't love me.
- I'm an inadequate lover.
- She must be having sex with someone else.
- She's selfish; she doesn't care about my sexual needs.
- She's frigid; it's got nothing to do with me.

The first is the most common misinterpretation and is extremely damaging, yet the woman often has no idea at all that this might be how her partner feels.

The woman in this couple is likely to interpret his regular desire for sex as:

- He doesn't love me; he only wants sex.
- There's something wrong with me because I don't enjoy some of the things he wants me to do.
- If I don't give him sex, he'll look for it somewhere else.
- He's selfish; he doesn't care about how I feel, that I'm tired, etc.
- He's a sex maniac.

As with her partner, the most common misinterpretation for the woman is that he doesn't really care about her as a person—she is just a body to satisfy his sexual needs.

Occasionally, some of these interpretations may be accurate, and if that's so, it's unlikely that reading a self-help book will be enough to help the couple address the serious issues facing them. More commonly, though, none of these interpretations is an accurate reflection of what the problems associated with mismatched libido are all about. Yet, without clarification, these misinterpretations persist and create more hurt and chaos, leading to the next phase of the anti-libido cycle.

Polarization

Although occasionally there are some couples in which one partner is obsessed with sex, or the other totally rejects it, in my experience, the majority of couples begin their relationship with normal but different levels and styles of sex drive. Over the years, the negative cycle that operates between a couple with mismatched libidos snowballs. The feelings of hurt, rejection, inadequacy, and anger percolate away, causing each to retreat even further from the other, and in retreating, each may take a more extreme position than he or she actually wants.

When the man has the higher libido, he may appear to be a sex maniac, but often, his frequent attempts to initiate sex are made on the basis that if he asks enough, he may get a positive response occasionally. Because she rarely if ever initiates sex, how does he know whether she might be interested unless he tries? In truth, if he knew they were going to have sex maybe once a week, he could relax and take the pressure off her.

In this instance, all the woman may see is that her partner is constantly harassing her for sex, so she has no idea that he would, in fact, be happy with less frequent sex. In her mind, his behavior merely confirms that he wants sex for physical release, so she doesn't understand that perhaps his feelings of emotional rejection are more important to him than the fact that he's not having sex.

The woman with low libido increasingly feels rejected as a person because the man seems preoccupied with sexual satisfaction, so she withdraws more and more from his advances. It becomes increasingly difficult for her to feel any pleasure at the thought of sex, because she sees sex as something for him, not for her. If she does "give in," he may believe that because she isn't responding to his physical caresses and reaching great heights of arousal and orgasm, she really doesn't love him, which just makes him feel more desperate.

And so it goes on.

Eventually, their positions are so polarized that any compromise seems impossible. Yet, is the situation really as bad as that? Hidden somewhere in all the conflict, hurt, and guilt are usually two normal, reasonable people who basically want the same thing—a caring relationship that includes a relaxed and stress-free sex life. Unfortunately, the increasing polarization of a couple at opposite ends of the sexual desire spectrum leads to increasing distance between them emotionally.

Isolation

Sadly, the conflict over sex can take its toll in other areas of the relationship. As each partner retreats even more, it can be a lot harder to help each other with daily chores, support each other, and be affectionate with each other.

Initially, the woman may avoid cuddling in case he interprets that as a sign that she's in the mood for sex. He tries to cuddle her as often as he can, partly for emotional reassurance, partly to test out his options. She may feel pressured by his insistence on cuddling, so she gives out more definite negative signals: turning her back on him, staying on the far side of the bed. As affection becomes more infrequent, if she does at times cuddle him, he has an "Aha!" reaction. "Gee, she seems to be in a good mood; she seems to like me tonight, so I think I'll try my luck." This confirms in her mind that he cuddles her only for sex, so she not only withdraws from cuddling that will lead to sex, she may also avoid smiling at him in case he wants to come and sit next to her . . . and so on.

After several years of this, the couple may lose even basic caring communication, such as eye contact, smiles, and goodbye kisses. They become two lonely, isolated people who are sometimes too afraid to even touch in bed at night, so that one or both cling uncomfortably close to the edge to avoid contact.

How can any relationship survive under this intense pressure?

Separation

It's hard to say how many couples separate because of differences in sexual desire, but certainly a lot do. At least some of these separations could be avoided if the negative cycle could be stopped early enough.

For some couples who come to sex therapy, it's already too late. At least one person has given up and has already decided that the marriage must end. In other cases, the gap between the partners' differing needs and expectations may simply be too great. Then the therapist can only help them separate with as little pain as possible.

For many couples, though, particularly those who seek help in the early stages of difficulty, the differences between them can be resolved. Perhaps not perfectly, perhaps not to the point where they have a great sex life, but well enough to give them the type of caring, contented sex life that reinforces rather than destroys their relationship.

CHAPTER 7

LIVING IN THE REAL WORLD

ALTHOUGH MOST COUPLES WHO ARE WORRIED ABOUT THE WOMAN'S LIBIDO are reacting to society's stereotype of sexual desire as a hot physical need, additional complicating factors sometimes make it even more unlikely that the couple will achieve the hoped-for fantasy sex life. These adverse influences may be as simple as sexual ignorance and lifestyle factors or as complex as distressing past histories, ongoing psychological difficulties, current relationship problems, and serious health problems.

ORDINARY LIVES

Couples who seek sex therapy are mostly ordinary people leading everyday lives. The complicating factors that add to their sexual worries are not strange or unusual but are issues that are part of the lives of many people in our communities.

Ignorance

Kathy and Gary

Kathy was clearly embarrassed as she tried to explain her problem to me. "I can't have an orgasm, and Gary says he's never been with a woman who couldn't climax before. He's been in two other relationships, and he says both of those women didn't have any trouble with coming during sex, so it must be that I'm having this problem because my parents are pretty conservative about sex. He's a decent guy; he doesn't want me not to enjoy sex; he doesn't want to be selfish like that."

Kathy went on to explain that she hadn't had much experience with sex, preferring to keep her early relationships nonsexual because of her upbringing. However, the relationship she had before she met Gary lasted 18 months and did become sexual, which she found very enjoyable. She always looked forward to sex and usually felt quite happy afterward, even if she was a bit shy about some of the things that her partner wanted to do.

When she met Gary, she was keen to have sex, but then Gary started asking her why she didn't come. She didn't know what to say to him because she hadn't realized there was anything wrong. Gary told her he knew she wasn't having orgasms because he couldn't feel anything when he was inside her, and he was sure he should feel her vagina grabbing his penis if she had an orgasm. Now, every time they have sex, he spends a long time trying to turn her on. He tries everything—hand stimulation, oral sex, a vibrator. She gets wet, so she knows she's getting aroused, but then it all gets to be too much, and he has to stop. Now she isn't interested in sex at all, because it just seems too much like hard work, and she didn't know what to do.

"What made sex enjoyable with your first partner?" I asked.

"I really liked the closeness, I enjoyed being kissed and stroked during foreplay, and when we had intercourse, I used to get this nice little tingly feeling . . ." she said somewhat wistfully.

"Was it like that when you and Gary began to have sex?"

"Yes," she said, "but not for a while now. How can this be happening, when Gary is such a considerate lover?"

Since the 1960s, sex education has been acknowledged to be an important part of a growing child's education. Many organizations have been established since then to develop suitable programs to prepare children for their future sexual relationships. In the early years, these programs focused exclusively on teaching young people how babies are made. Over time, as the frequency of teenage pregnancy rose, contraceptive advice was included, although not without a lot of debate and opposition. Many adults were concerned that this knowledge would encourage teenage sexual activity, because fear of pregnancy was thought to be a major influence in controlling it. In the end, the sheer weight of the problem forced a move toward more explicit information. However, information about how to make sex pleasurable was still excluded, and it remains a forbidden topic in most sex education programs.

Today, we certainly know more about the mechanics of sex than previous generations did. However, because sex is usually portrayed in idealized ways, many of the details of normal sexual function are glossed over. Though it would be rare to find a man who didn't know that women have clitorises or a woman who didn't know about orgasms, there remain significant areas of ignorance that affect people's ability to have satisfying sexual relationships.

Gary is a good example of someone who means well but whose ignorance about female sexuality has created a problem where one did not previously exist. The common belief that when a woman comes to orgasm during intercourse, she should have strong vaginal contractions that her partner feels as pressure on his penis arose out of Masters and Johnson's original research, in which they observed contractions of the vaginal wall during orgasm. However, that became translated into the belief that the contractions should be felt by the woman's partner, implying that if he didn't feel them, she couldn't be having an orgasm. The truth is that the strength of female orgasm varies from time to time and from woman to woman. Orgasms are always described in books and movies in superlative terms, so there is often no understanding that they range from very mild, almost like a sigh, to quite strong, as simulated by Meg Ryan in the famous scene in *When Harry Met Sally*. Think of orgasm as varying along a 10-point scale. Although the partner may be aware of the woman's orgasm if she comes during intercourse, the chances are that he will have no way of knowing when she has a softer, milder orgasm. Similarly, women can make sex very stressful for themselves if they believe the old chestnut that has been around for some time—that climaxing is so mind-blowing that if you're not sure whether you've had an orgasm, you can't possibly have had one. If women are waiting to feel rivers of fire coursing through their body, culminating in flames of ecstasy burning through them as they ride the waves of orgasmic pleasure, an awful lot of them are going to be sorely disappointed. A major downside of this misinformation is that they are ignoring the more subtle cues that they are becoming aroused and may totally miss the pleasant, warm feeling that is orgasm. Many women shut off any pleasure during foreplay by their constant preoccupation with whether they are feeling anything yet, whether it will happen this time, whether this or that feeling means they are going to come, and so on.

Probably half of the women who consult me because they believe they are not having orgasms usually discover that, in fact, they have been having them for some time. Ask yourself, do I find stimulation of my breasts and clitoris pleasurable or annoying? When it is pleasurable, does it produce warm or tingly feelings? During intercourse, do I feel nothing at all, a neutral sensation that is just awareness of the skin contact, or an enjoyable feeling that is tickly or tingly or indicates muscle tension? Why does the stimulation stop: Because I feel increasingly irritated, or because it feels as if I have had enough? And when I have finished, do I feel tense and frustrated, congested in the pelvic area, or relaxed and sleepy? If you have found the stimulation pleasant and enjoyable, and you feel calm, relaxed, contented, and/or sleepy afterward, there has been some type of orgasmic release. Becoming aroused and not having an orgasm leaves a woman uncomfortable and tense.

A good deal of ignorance also exists about how a woman behaves during orgasm. I saw one couple in which the man believed that his wife lacked libido and didn't enjoy sex because she didn't make any sort of hot noises when she initiated sex or claimed she had come. After all, that's what women did in all the erotic movies he had seen. His partner was a woman who looked forward to sex, liked to experiment with sex toys and different techniques, and was comfortable with masturbation, either on her own or with her partner present, yet her husband dragged her to many therapists over the years to find out why she had a problem getting aroused. By the time I saw her, she was so fed up with his pressure that she had totally lost interest in sex and had moved out of the bedroom.

This type of ignorance influences both what the couple tries to do during sex and how they feel about themselves. Gary's insistence that Kathy could not be having orgasms caused her to doubt her own experience. He persisted with what he thought should be arousing techniques to the point that sex became an endurance feat that was irritating and exhausting. Previously, Kathy had enjoyed intercourse, and those nice, tingly feelings she was experiencing were indeed orgasms, even if relatively mild. His well-intentioned but ill-informed pressure to produce his version of orgasm meant that sex became a stressful, unpleasant activity that Kathy ultimately preferred to avoid.

Sometimes, it's hard to distinguish between plain ignorance and unrealistic expectations. For example, if either partner doesn't appreciate that it is normal for women to find breast and genital stimulation annoying when they are tired, stressed, or preoccupied, is this an example of lack of knowledge or of trying to live in a fantasy world? A worrying situation that occurs with many couples is that even when the woman tells her partner that this is how it is for her, he doesn't believe her and continues to stimulate her because he believes she should enjoy it.

Similarly, is it ignorance or is it unrealistic expectations that make some people believe that a woman should be able to want sex and become aroused easily without any intimate contact beforehand? I don't mean just sensual foreplay. A woman I once saw for low libido said that her husband worked long hours at a demanding job and would unwind when he came home from work by spending hours playing computer games. She would often watch TV alone; then at some point, he would come to her and want her to go to bed for sex. This couple had a generally good relationship, but he genuinely believed she had a problem because she would often refuse his advances.

Another man consulted me about infrequent sex. He was a wealthy man who had achieved success by virtue of his workaholic personality. His wife complained about how little time they spent together, so I suggested that that could have something to do with why they weren't having sex very often. The man loved his wife and wanted to please her but was perplexed when the solution he came up with didn't work. He examined his busy schedule and decided that on Monday and Thursday evenings, he could set aside an hour or so when they could get together for sex. He wondered what was wrong with her when it turned out that this wasn't enough time for her to enjoy sex.

Whether a couple's sexual problem is due to ignorance or to unrealistic expectations, sometimes it is easily solved by correcting the misinformation. But where do you get access to information that will address all your doubts and questions when most of the books on sex don't discuss such mundane issues and continue to portray sex in fantasy terms?

On the other hand, trying to reverse the damage done to a woman's sexuality may not be a straightforward matter of sex education. Building the woman's confidence in her own perception of her sexual experiences can take time and practice. It means starting with the assumption that whatever she feels is valid for her, and then identifying what feels pleasant or arousing for her, even if this is quite different from what she or her partner may have read or believe is normal for most women.

Lifestyle

Nicole and Jeff

Nicole had only just sat down in my office when she began to cry. "I don't know what to do; I don't know what's wrong with me," she told me when she was able to regain her composure.

She explained that she and Jeff have been married for seven years and have two children, ages 6 and 4. Nicole describes Jeff as a good man who works hard to support his family, and she loves him very much. Unfortunately, Jeff's income is low, so Nicole, a nurse, had to get a job to give the children the best possible opportunities. Neither she nor Jeff has family living nearby to help, so she works nights when Jeff is home to care for the children.

"I feel so guilty," Nicole said. "Jeff works so hard, he takes all the overtime he can get, and when he's home with the kids, he does what he can so I don't have to do too much during the day. I think about having sex, but it just doesn't happen. When I know he wants it, I try to avoid it by telling him I've got something to do. Sometimes we don't have sex for a couple of months. He says he understands, as we are both so damned tired, but I know he still wants it, whereas I just don't. Jeff tries to get me interested by telling me it's a great way to relax. What's wrong with me that I mostly find it irritating?"

There is a surprisingly large portion of our society that seems to believe that sex should be the one thing that remains unaffected by day-to-day worries. Perhaps this notion comes from the movies, where the hero and heroine suffer all manner of amazing hardships and overcome tremendous obstacles as they journey through the plotline, yet they still have the time and energy for fantastic sex. Or perhaps it comes from society's belief that everyone is entitled to a fulfilling, enriched life. If life is in reality less rewarding and more of a hassle than we feel we deserve, we cling to the hope that at least sex should give us what we want. Unfortunately, it doesn't work like that, but the expectation that it should can produce unreasonable pressure on one or both partners.

Nicole and Jeff are typical of young parents who are juggling family responsibilities and work demands. Without time together to relax, catch up with each other, and enjoy their relationship, it shouldn't be surprising that although Jeff is still interested in sex, Nicole can't be bothered. But when weeks pass with no sex, it's no wonder Nicole feels guilty if she believes she's letting Jeff down. Both Nicole and Jeff, who came to the second session, were relieved to learn that there was nothing wrong with either of them, and they happily restarted their sex life using the principles of relationship sex that were introduced in chapter 5.

Many couples find themselves under pressure from the demands of everyday life. In Faye and Stan's case, Faye feels interested in sex sometimes but not when Stan wants it. He is a taxi driver and is keen for sex when he gets home in the early hours of the morning. He believes that sex should be better for Faye then, too, because they have more privacy and time than later in the day, when it suits Faye. He can't understand why she isn't turned on by him waking her up for sex, and when she does go along with it, he is disappointed that she wants only "quickies."

Another couple, Brenda and Peter, clearly have the odds against them when it comes to regaining their previously active and satisfying sex life, at least in the short term. They have three very young children, are in financial difficulty, and are living in a trailer home with no private room. Brenda is physically tired, stressed by trying to make do with their limited income, and inhibited by the lack of privacy with their children sleeping nearby. In addition, she has always found the messiness of sex somewhat off-putting. This wasn't a problem in the past, when she could have a quick shower after lovemaking, but in the trailer home, the couple has to wait until the children are asleep to have some time to themselves. This means that sex takes place only late in the evening, and if Brenda wants to have a shower, she has to leave the trailer to use the communal facilities. Ususually there's no way she feels like doing this, particularly in cold or wet weather. No wonder sex seems like too much of a hassle!

Couples such as these have a lifestyle problem rather than a sexual problem. Quite reasonably, the various stresses they are confronting have an impact on their sex life. For example, on a very practical level, when would Nicole and Jeff find the time for sex? They are rarely at home together, and when they are, there are the children to consider and the usual household chores to be done. They barely have time to sit down and chat, let alone relax enough for Nicole to tune in to any lingering sexual feelings.

Although it's disappointing and frustrating that lifestyle can so effectively shred a couple's sex life, it doesn't mean that anyone has a sexual dysfunction. Generally, I find that under these circumstances, the man's libido is more likely to survive, and he will see sex as a stress reducer. He may nevertheless find he has little energy for sex with his wife and prefer to masturbate. The woman, however, is likely to feel absolutely no sexual desire at all, and even when the couple goes on vacation, she may prefer to catch up on her sleep rather than catch up on sex. So what do couples in this situation do—just resign themselves to misery?

It's true that couples are unlikely to achieve anywhere near their hoped-for sex life while their everyday lives are so busy and stressful, but it's up to them whether they have a miserable time or do their best to adapt to their situation as much as possible. Many couples experience long periods when they feel burdened by ongoing problems. Life can throw up a tremendous variety of challenges: Caring for aged parents, having a disabled child who needs constant care, having to work long hours at a demanding job, and juggling family and household responsibilities while holding down a job all take their toll on a person's energy and sense of well-being.

We can shrug our shoulders in good-natured resignation if these stresses last for a brief period and if sex is interrupted to a limited degree, but for some couples, the problems are unrelenting. These are the couples for whom the concept of relationship sex is particularly relevant.

If the partners' emotional relationship is sound, their sexual relationship can provide them with some intimate time when they can give each other support as they struggle to cope with problems that at times may threaten to overwhelm them. Quiet, comforting, gentle sex can offer both partners the reassurance they seek. But under long-term difficult circumstances, even low-key sex is likely to be sporadic.

Sometimes, there are practical issues to take into consideration that require a commonsense solution. In our idealization of sex, we gloss over some unglamorous but very real irritations that can be turnoffs for some women. For Brenda, the messiness of sex was part of the reason that she preferred to avoid it late at night, as she had no accessible shower facilities. Over the years, I have asked women whether this aspect of sex bothers them, and there is a three-way split in the answers. There are some women who are totally oblivious to any discomfort arising from their own secretions or their partner's semen, others who recognize that they prefer to routinely clean themselves in some way after sex but don't give it any real thought, and a third group who dislike the messiness but don't feel comfortable acknowledging it and taking practical steps to address it. It seems that there is a general expectation that sex should be so overwhelmingly wonderful that considerations such as the woman not liking the cold wetness between her legs or on the sheets is somehow heresy and a sign that she has serious inhibitions.

Given the earlier discussion of individual differences, it's obvious that things that bother some women aren't a problem for others. An almost infinite array of practical turnoffs affect some people, yet the same things may even be part of what turns others on: a sweaty body, stale breath, an uncomfortable bed, people sleeping in the next room, a cold room, a hot room, lights on, lights off, and so on. Even settings that are meant to be romantic aren't always appealing: I've seen women who hate the thought of sex on the beach because sand can get into some very uncomfortable places. One woman hated the cold, yet when she made love with her nightclothes on, she felt literally tied up, so unplanned sex was never an option during winter because she needed the room to be warmed first.

No matter what the particular irritants are, everyone has the right to their harmless idiosyncrasies without being labeled as inhibited or dysfunctional. Accepting the situation as reasonable and coming up with practical solutions can make a difference in a woman's willingness to have sex. In Brenda's case, she found that routinely keeping a sponge, a towel, and a jug of water in the trailer meant that she could easily wash herself, and then she inserted a tampon until she could shower in the morning. Perhaps it's not romantic, but it meant that sex became a more pleasant option when she knew she could settle down to sleep more comfortably.

Some men are offended if their partner complains about breath or body odor. However, if he refuses to do something about it, the low frequency of sex in their relationship is as much his responsibility as it is his partner's. Most men, though, are pleased when their partner gives practical suggestions that help her feel more inclined to have sex.

Life Events

Melanie and Nick

"We've been through so much together, and I feel sorry for Nick. I know he gets frustrated, but I don't think he understands how difficult it is for me," said Melanie as she outlined the hurdles she and Nick have had to overcome during their 12 years of marriage. Melanie went on to tell me that prior to their marriage, sex was good for both of them. Unfortunately, Melanie's mother was diagnosed with cancer two months before the wedding and died only days afterward. Then Nick's father was killed in a car accident some months later. Melanie had a miscarriage two years into the marriage and didn't conceive again. Later, she entered an in vitro fertilization program, and it took two years for her to become pregnant. She was sick constantly throughout the pregnancy and had a difficult delivery. The baby, Grace, was hard to settle, so Melanie didn't get a lot of sleep.

The delivery left Melanie with vaginal scarring. An attempt to repair it wasn't a complete success, and because further surgery was likely to lead to more scar tissue and adhesions, her gynecologist advised against it. As a result, she found intercourse to be uncomfortable at best and painful at worst. All of this took its toll on her libido, and she wished Nick could lose his sex drive as well.

Nick frowned and sat forward as he spoke. "I do understand that she has all these problems, but what am I supposed to do? I'm only in my thirties—does this mean I should accept that my sex life is over? Sure, I can masturbate, and I do, but that's pretty lonely. I mean, it gives me physical relief, but that's not all I need. And when I ask her to do it for me, give me a hand or mouth job, she isn't open to doing that either."

"He seems to think I'm being unreasonable, that he's missing out because of me," replied Melanie. "He doesn't understand that I'm missing out, too. I miss feeling hot for sex, and I miss having orgasms. At least he feels randy and can come, even if it is only with masturbation. I'd give anything to have a night of passion again."

Life can sometimes be very good: a secure job, enough money to get by, a loving relationship, a happy family life, lots of friends. Everything seems to be going according to plan, and the couple takes their sex life for granted. It's easy to desire each other, sex happens regularly, and both are content and satisfied with what they share in their sexual relationship. However, life has a way of taking a sudden turn that can disturb this contented existence. Events such as the death of a loved one, the loss of a job, moving to another area, and even the birth of a much-wanted baby can put pressure on one or both partners and disrupt the usual easy pattern of their sex life.

Melanie and Nick began married life with a distressing series of life events: the death of her mother and his father in the first few months of marriage, then a miscarriage a year after that. It's not surprising that she lost some of her usual exuberance for life and that this began to take a toll on her libido.

Pauline and Andrew are another couple whose sex life suffered when problems they had no control over arose in their lives. They sustained a solid marriage for over 32 years, and Andrew's tendency to ejaculate rapidly didn't hinder them from developing a sexual relationship that both found enjoyable. Then, two things happened that threw them into disarray. When Pauline began to go through menopause, she experienced a number of the symptoms that many women are fortunate enough not to have, including hot flashes, lethargy, and irritability. At the same time, one of their sons went through a very messy, high-conflict divorce, and for a while, it seemed that they might lose contact with their much-loved grandchildren. Pauline's worry about the welfare of her son and grandchildren preoccupied her constantly. She began to experience symptoms of depression and to withdraw from Andrew. Their previously robust sex life was reduced to unsatisfying encounters once every few months.

There is some interesting research from a large Australian study that found that menopause alone usually does not lead to loss of libido, but if there are significant stresses in the woman's life at that time, the combination can cause her libido to wane. These stresses can include relationship problems with her husband, which previously she could cope with sufficiently to maintain their sexual relationship, as well as life events such as the family problems that overwhelmed Pauline.

Life events affect a person's sexuality in a number of ways. Distressing occurrences such as the death of a loved one or the loss of a job trigger feelings of grief, anger, despair, or depression. These feelings can be overwhelming and crush the person's sense of well-being for long periods of time. It's difficult to feel energetic and lighthearted enough for passionate sex and erotic games when the mind and body are slowed down by the struggle to come to terms with a new and possibly unexpected development.

It's not just the direct emotional consequences of a life event that can affect the couple's sex life. Some events may mean an adjustment in lifestyle. The loss of one elderly parent may mean that the remaining parent needs more time and care. A change in employment may mean trips away from home. The incarceration of a family member may mean social embarrassment as well as time for visits to the jail. A son or daughter's divorce may lead to more time looking after grandchildren. Lack of time to relax, disruption of usual social outings, and changes in daily routine can all interrupt a couple's usual pattern of sexual activity.

A life event that most couples experience is the birth of a baby, and of course, no matter how wanted the child is, his arrival can seriously interfere with a couple's sex life. Parents frequently bemoan their loss of passion once a bundle of joy enters their lives. I became interested in this problem in the early 1970s and chose loss of sexual desire and enjoyment after childbirth as the topic for my doctoral dissertation. There were a number of theories around at the time that offered explanations for this problem. One suggested that birth was like orgasm, so the woman was satiated and didn't need sex for a long time afterward; strangely, when I mention this theory in workshops, some women laugh uncontrollably. Another theory put forward the view that when a woman becomes a mother, she isn't comfortable seeing herself as a sexual being, because this interferes with her view of herself as a Madonna figure.

My own research came to some much more down-to-earth conclusions: After three studies, I found that the factor most associated with postnatal loss of libido was fatigue! This conclusion shouldn't have been at all surprising, but what was surprising was that a research project was needed to establish it. I found that about 50 percent of new mothers reported being less interested in sex in the 12 months after childbirth than was usual for them, and 25 percent reported loss of enjoyment. This difference in the desire and enjoyment figures was intriguing, as it gave an early clue to the fact that the main problem for many women is to actually feel like having sex in the first place, even though many women with low libido are able to enjoy it once they get into it.

Whatever the life event a woman has gone through, if it triggers loss of libido, there isn't necessarily a quick fix that can restore her former level of sexual desire and enjoyment. Some events, such as having a child, dramatically change the woman's life for the long term, and if she has other children, it may be years before she feels like her old self again. Other events—such as adjusting to new responsibilities at work—are short-lived, so there is eventually a sense that the problem is over or has been dealt with and that life should get back to normal. What is critical to the recovery of her libido is the way in which the couple copes with the situation while her sex drive is depressed.

If the couple is realistic and accepting of the situation and can adapt their sexual relationship accordingly, without guilt or recriminations, as the effects of the life event pass or settle down, their sex life should begin to bounce back. A word of caution, though: Recovery of lost libido is usually not like turning on a switch so that everything is immediately back to normal. Instead, progress is usually gradual. The woman may unexpectedly feel some old feelings of desire and be more like her old self one night, but it may not last, and her libido may disappear again for several days or weeks. Hopefully, over time, these episodes of feeling good will happen more often and last for longer periods, but the up-and-down effect is quite normal.

If the woman worries, however, that after one good episode, her partner will assume that everything is okay and he can expect their old pattern to return, she may hold back on expressing her sexual feelings. Because she can't guarantee that they will continue, she doesn't want to give her partner false hope. This will have the effect of slowing the recovery process because she won't allow herself to explore and enjoy what is right for her at that time. She needs the freedom to respond according to what is possible on any particular occasion. It can do a lot for her self-confidence to have occasional flashes of passion, so she needs to be able to savor them when they occur, even if it feels unfair when they disappear again.

Of more concern, however, is the couple who is unable to understand

and accept the changes in their sex life during the period when the stressful event is having the most impact. If the woman feels guilty, or the man feels ignored, resentful, or irritated, and their sex life becomes an issue between them, the anti-libido cycle kicks in with full force. Instead of their sexual relationship providing comfort and support during a difficult time, it becomes a problem in its own right, and instead of the partners approaching sex with confidence, the atmosphere changes to one of tension and even hostility. The sad effect of this is that even when the life event is long over, the consequences for their sexual relationship linger on and may even lead to further deterioration. How can any sexual feelings begin to flower in such a harsh climate?

If the couple can adopt the concept of relationship sex and allow their sex life to ebb and flow in response to their life stresses, it has a better chance of returning to its former state.

Your Personal Difficulties

Ruth and John

Ruth was very distressed. "I love John, but I just can't keep doing it anymore. I've tried, I've really tried, but it makes me feel sick. It wasn't like this in the early years, but in the past 12 months, I can't stand for him to touch me. He's so hurt and confused."

When I asked Ruth what she thought was the reason that she had switched off sex, she said, "I think it's got something to do with my childhood, but it's confusing to me, too, because it didn't seem to worry me so much before."

Ruth went on to talk about her sexual abuse by her father. He started to come into her bedroom at night when she was about 6, and the abuse went on for many years. It began with fondling but developed into demands that she stimulate him manually and orally. When she was a teenager, a teacher talked about sexual abuse, and this gave Ruth the courage to tell her father that if he touched her again, she'd tell the teacher. He stopped, and she didn't tell anyone until she met John years later.

"He's been wonderful, very gentle, very caring, and I was able to enjoy sex with him. He is the only man I've trusted. Now it's all come back, and he tries to talk to me about it and tells me he's not my father, but it doesn't help," Ruth said.

"What changed 12 months ago?" I asked quietly.

"I began thinking about it more and more, going over what he did in my mind, wondering how he could have done it. I got so angry about it that a few months ago I confronted him, and of course, he denied it at first, but I told him I didn't care whether he admitted it or not, I knew what he had done. Mom is devastated, she says she had no idea, but she is still with him. When I look at Carlie, my own daughter, I can't understand how anyone could do what he did."

"How old is Carlie?" I asked.

"She's 7 now," Ruth replied.

"So a year ago, she turned 6—the age you were when the abuse started."

"Yes," Ruth whispered, "I looked at her on her birthday and thought about how young and vulnerable she was, how sweet and innocent, and I thought of someone touching her like my father touched me, and the rage almost choked me. And I haven't been able to stop thinking about it since then."

∽

Although long-term consequences of childhood sexual abuse vary from person to person, a past history of abuse can be associated with adult sexual difficulties. Ruth had done very well for many years in her relationship with John, despite her history of sexual abuse by her father. John was understanding and supportive, and Ruth was able to develop a level of trust that enabled her to separate her past experience from sex with him. But, as sometimes happens, when Ruth's daughter reached the age that her own abuse had begun, Ruth was able to realize how young, fragile, and innocent she had been when her father abused her. Her rage at her father and her fears for her daughter overwhelmed her and cut her off from John so that sex became impossible. Ruth needed time to sort through these complex emotions before she could restore her sexual relationship with John.

It can take time and patience to work out whether past abuse is related to current sexual worries. Sometimes, as in Ruth's case, the connection soon becomes clear—the woman may be experiencing flashbacks or strong feelings during sex that are reminiscent of the abuse. In other cases, the connection may be more subtle. Perhaps the woman is fine during sex unless a specific trigger occurs, such as a particular touch or smell. It may be that relatively simple strategies, such as keeping the lights on, avoiding specific triggers, or softly talking with her partner so that she remembers she is now with someone she trusts, will make a difference in her willingness to have sex. For some victims of abuse, however, it's beneficial to find a competent therapist to help them deal with the past before expecting any change in sexual desire.

The relationship between psychological problems and low libido is not always straightforward. Because there is a common belief that low libido is caused by complex psychological difficulties, it's often tempting to assume that if such a problem exists, it must be relevant to the woman's sexuality. This is particularly true if there is a past history of sexual, physical, or emotional abuse.

Jenny was molested by her older brother when she was a child, and when she consulted a therapist about her low libido in her relationship with Matthew, the therapist zeroed in on her past and ignored the present in her attempts to help Jenny understand and resolve her sexual problem. There is a school of thought among some therapists that a victim of child abuse should express her anger and confront her offender or, according to other therapists, forgive her offender. In Jenny's case, the therapist encouraged her to confront her brother and tell her parents, which caused great upheaval in the family. After initial denials, her brother admitted what he had done. This led to a major row in the family, and her brother became estranged from them. Jenny's parents' attitude toward her changed, with her father angrily saying that he didn't know why she had to bring it up now, when it had happened so long ago. In the end, she hadn't resolved any of the family issues, and she still didn't want sex.

It is my view that these rigid beliefs about therapy that are not backed up by rigorous research are quite dangerous and, in fact, constitute abuse by the therapist when they are insisted upon in the therapeutic process. The therapist's responsibility is to explore what is right for each client and respect her choices, because clearly, to do otherwise is to replay the childhood abuse scenario. There are many cases in which it is either too dangerous to confront an offender, or the victim prefers not to for reasons that are entirely valid to her. In Jenny's case, she didn't want to disclose her brother's abuse because she knew it would be devastating to her parents, and this proved to be the case. Also, in the end, the abuse had nothing to do with Jenny's low libido. Gentle questioning revealed that she found intercourse painful and boring because Matthew experienced inhibited ejaculation and would take more than 30 minutes of penile thrusting to come. In Matthew's case, his inhibited ejaculation was related to his practice of masturbating daily, and his time to ejaculation improved significantly when he limited this activity. Jenny's interest in sex was gradually restored.

A range of traumatic past events may need to be addressed as part of sex therapy, but careful analysis needs to be done before making any conclusions that there is definitely a causal connection. These past events include diverse experiences such as parental alcohol abuse, family attitudes about sex, the death of significant people at critical developmental stages, and even being bullied at school. Additionally, it may be that if there are long-term consequences for the woman's sexuality, they may not all be entirely reversible. The concept of appreciating what you can do rather than beating yourself up for what you can't becomes very important in these kinds of situation.

Not all psychological problems in adulthood are caused by a traumatic past. One of the most common psychological disorders of modern times is major depression, which may occur because of biological vulnerability to depression or as a reaction to distressing or difficult periods in life. One of the symptoms of depression is loss of libido, which makes sense given that sexual desire and enjoyment, particularly for women, is generally an expression of well-being. Other psychological problems, such as eating disorders, substance abuse, and anxiety disorders (such as panic disorder), can all affect the ability to feel sexually interested. Struggling with specific issues such as infertility may also depress libido.

Sometimes, the connection between a psychological disorder and low libido isn't immediately obvious. Jodi was a very capable young woman who was in a good relationship with Ben. Her libido took a serious dive when they moved in together. This is not uncommon, because once a couple moves in together, many of the behaviors that help a woman turn on may decrease. In Jodi's case, however, her inability to relax and her need for order were symptoms of obsessive compulsive disorder. Although many women like their homes to be neat and tidy and get exasperated if things get too messy, Jodi needed the apartment to be absolutely spotless and organized, or she felt agitated. She couldn't rest until the whole apartment was just right, and of course, this was a neverending task. Minor disarray, such as cushions left at the wrong angle on the sofa or crumbs on the benches in the kitchen, annoyed her, and she would have to fix things to her satisfaction. As a result, she had neither the time nor the energy for sex.

In all these cases, along with exploring the usual unrealistic expectations about sex and the misunderstandings about individual and gender differences, the woman's personal emotional troubles will need to be addressed. It would be beneficial to consult a competent mental health professional who has a good understanding of the sexual and psychological issues involved.

Your Partner's Personal Difficulties

Erin and Steve

Steve got straight to the point. "We came to see you twenty years ago, and, frankly, you weren't at all helpful. Erin has absolutely no libido, and she is hopeless at sex, and you tried to tell me she was perfectly normal. But I've taken her to other sex therapists and none of them have been able to help, so I thought we'd try you again!"

I looked at Erin. She was sitting calmly, letting Steve talk.

"There is obviously something seriously wrong, but no one has been able to work it out," Steve went on. "Erin's family were very conservative, so maybe that's where she got her hang-ups from, or else something happened that she just won't talk about . . ."

He continued in this vein for a while, and I thought it was time Erin put in her point of view.

"How do you see this sexual issue?" I asked.

"I was 17 when I met Steve at a church group," Erin began. "He's nine years older than me, and I admired his values, his faith, his commitment to social justice. We were both virgins and now I realize I was incredibly naïve. Neither of us believed in sex before marriage, but we sure enjoyed doing almost everything else. We got engaged, and I was certainly looking forward to the honeymoon. I realize I wasn't very knowledgeable about sex, but I thoroughly enjoyed it. I even climaxed when Steve caressed my clitoris. But as the days passed, I knew Steve was upset about something, and when we got home, he finally let me have it. He told me how disappointed he was in me, how I hadn't done anything to please him, and it just went on and on. I was totally devastated, and I've been trying to please him ever since, but nothing I do is right, and, I admit, in the end I gave up. Every so often, we would see a therapist, we'd try the different ideas, but nothing has helped."

"That's the trouble," Steve interjected angrily, "she doesn't try.

She doesn't consider me at all, she's very selfish, and I try to get her to talk to me about her problems but she won't."

Erin sighed. "I do try to talk to him, but if I don't tell him what he wants to hear—that I do have a problem, that our bad sex life is all my fault—he just goes on and on. If I try to tell him what I would like, he accuses me of being uncaring and insensitive. I know it hurts him that I can't give him what he wants, but I don't know what to do about it."

I started to talk about normal female sexuality, individual differences, and realistic expectations of sex, but Steve interrupted.

"That's the stuff you told us last time—it's rubbish! If it was up to Erin, we'd be lucky to have sex twice a week, and it would be all over in half an hour. That's not normal sex! She says she loves me, but she only initiates sex some of the time, and it's obviously an effort for her to do the things I like. I've bought her lingerie, but she rarely puts it on unless I ask her."

I made the comment that it's not always possible to have great sex everyday, particularly when both partners are working full-time and they have a teenage family still living at home.

"Why not? Love is a spiritual experience, and that should translate into our sex life. It shouldn't be an effort. Okay, I admit that what I want may be ideal, but surely we should at least be striving for it. Erin doesn't try at all, and I'm now in my 40s—she's making me miss out on a good sex life."

The sad thing about the case of Erin and Steve was that Erin was actually a very sexual and sensual person; she just couldn't compete with Steve's idealized beliefs about sex in a loving relationship. She certainly had a sex drive in the early years of their marriage, and she still wished to find a way of pleasing Steve so that they could both enjoy sex. In our early sessions, I encouraged them to start with what helped Erin want and enjoy sex, and she was quickly able to identify triggers that helped her feel like having sex and then become aroused and come to orgasm. However, when she happily reported this progress in our sessions, Steve's response was always that she was making no progress at all and that what they had been doing could hardly be called satisfactory sex. He believed that I was taking Erin's side and was probably anti-male.

After several difficult and draining sessions for all, it was obvious that sex therapy was not going to resolve this couple's problems. Because Steve wouldn't acknowledge his role in their unhappiness, and Erin couldn't transform herself into the sex partner he wanted, they were at a dead end. Ultimately, I saw Erin on her own for a couple of sessions to explore her options. Despite his dominating and controlling personality, Erin found that Steve could be sweet, kind, and generous in other ways, and this, combined with her religious beliefs, meant that she found it difficult to contemplate divorce. We spent our time on bolstering her self-esteem (she was not frigid or inadequate because she couldn't fulfill Steve's sexual needs) and assertiveness (she could continue to communicate her own feelings about what was happening and not allow herself to be pressured into performing to keep Steve happy).

Anne's husband, Richard, also had an idealized perception of a sexual relationship; he craved constant affection from Anne and wanted sex on at least a daily basis. Unlike Steve, however, Richard needed sex to cope with his depression and feelings of low self-worth. He wasn't worried about what the couple did during sex as long as he felt wanted and needed, and the good feeling he got from coming to orgasm gave him temporary relief from his bad feelings. Richard was dependent on sex to cope.

It's difficult to know what words to use to describe a person whose sexual desire is constant and demanding. The term *sex addiction* is one that has been used since the mid-1980s, but I have difficulty with this because it conjures up images of a sex-crazed maniac who stalks the streets desperate for his next "fix," like a drug addict. Just as some people who regularly use and abuse drugs and alcohol deny their problems by rejecting the label of *addict* or *alcoholic*, many people who require regular sexual release in order to cope reject the notion that they are addicted to sex. A further problem with the term *sex addiction* is that in popular literature now, it is used to refer to people who seek sex from numerous partners. Stories in magazines usually focus on the number of lovers an "addict" has had in an effort to satisfy the craving for sex.

Though this may be a genuine clinical phenomenon, I am more concerned here with people who have high sexual needs within a relationship. There are people who are dependent on arousal and orgasm, either through masturbation or with their partner, and do not seek sexual release with other people. As with alcohol use, there is a distinction between *want* and *need*. Many people may want sex several times a week or even daily, but it isn't a major problem for them if it doesn't happen that often. Sure, there may be some level of sexual frustration, but it doesn't dominate the person or preoccupy his thoughts.

A person who needs sex, who is sexually dependent, is someone who finds it increasingly difficult to cope without regular masturbation or sex. By far, the majority of cases I have seen are men. A man will say he can't sleep at night without sex, or he can't concentrate on his work; and in more extreme cases, he may have to go to the men's room to masturbate while at work just to deal with the demands of the day. When sexual feelings are experienced in this way, they are triggered by nonsexual factors, such as stress, anxiety, and depression. Arousal and orgasm are powerful feelings that can produce a state of relaxation, even euphoria. During adolescence, masturbation may be used initially in a quite harmless way to overcome boredom, sleeplessness, or feeling down. Over time, this association strengthens so that the person becomes "hooked" on this method of coping with bad feelings.

There are, of course, different levels of dependency. Most people are likely to experience the need for sex when they need comfort, reassurance, and so on. Generally, though, we know that this is why we want sex on that occasion, and it isn't our usual reason for seeking it. Also, on those occasions, we find that arousal is more muted, and we are more tuned in to the emotional/sensual aspects of sex. The dependent person, however, experiences a strong, persistent sexual feeling that compels him toward sexual release, and orgasm is his major focus. In general, I would regard a person as sexually dependent if he:

- Experiences regular, persistent sexual needs that tend to be stronger when he is under emotional pressure
- Can't cope without sexual release and becomes agitated, angry, tense, or preoccupied with sexual feelings if there is no opportunity for orgasm when the "need" is there
- Finds that the sexual need sometimes interferes with daily life—that satisfying it can be more important than other things, such as getting to work on time or keeping up to date with regular chores
- Expects his partner to have sex based on his need, with little or no consideration for her feelings, and uses various types of emotional manipulation to get those needs met

Unfortunately, I have found that sexually dependent people are usually reluctant to acknowledge that they have a problem, preferring to blame their partners, as in "There wouldn't be a problem if she would give me sex."

As in the situation with Erin and Steve, Anne found that counseling aimed at improving her self-esteem (she was not unreasonable because she could not meet Richard's high level of sexual needs) and assertiveness (she could calmly and confidently communicate her own feelings about what was happening and why she wouldn't always have sex on demand) was quite helpful. At the same time, Richard was prepared to acknowledge that he was quite depressed and had been for many years, and I referred him to a therapist who was experienced in such cases.

A quite different type of partner problem is shown in the case of Elizabeth and Martin. Elizabeth had always had a strong sex drive and was quite comfortable with a variety of sexual techniques. She had not been in a relationship for five years prior to meeting Martin and had masturbated regularly during that time. She was confused about her decreasing libido over the 10 months of her relationship with Martin, who in many ways was a good lover. But Martin had a particular sexual need that made Elizabeth uncomfortable. He initially introduced his fixation as something different to try in foreplay, but as the weeks went by, he asked for it on every occasion. Martin needed to spend time viewing Elizabeth's vulva; he wanted her to lie quite still with her legs spread while he sat looking at her for several minutes. I never interviewed Martin, but my guess is that this fetish developed during years of masturbating to pictures of women in this position, which are the typical photos in some men's magazines. Elizabeth's sexual desire decreased not specifically because of Martin's fetish but because he needed her to indulge it every time they had sex, which meant that sex was always about his needs and not hers, and because he told her there was something wrong with her because she was uncomfortable with it, which demonstrated a blatant disrespect for her sexuality while he expected respect for his own.

An almost infinite variety of sexual needs and attractions exists in the human species. At times, I think I must have come across every possible variation in my 30 years as a sex therapist, and then I'll come across something new. These sexual compulsions are known as paraphilias and can be broadly divided into two categories: a dependence on or preference for a specific object for sexual arousal, such as shoes, leather, women's underwear, plaster casts, and so on; and a specific situation, such as exhibiting the penis, or spying on women in intimate situations, such as using the toilet and undressing. Most paraphiliacs are male, and the strength of the compulsion varies from case to case. In mild cases, a man occasionally seeks out his particular interest but isn't bothered if the opportunity doesn't arise, and most typically, he has good sexual relationships with partners. At the other end of the scale are men who regularly spend significant time on their sexual rituals, at least weekly and perhaps daily, and this may mean they are not interested in relationships with partners. Surprisingly, however, a large number of men who have paraphilias conduct their rituals in secret and maintain relationships with their partners, although there may be some sexual difficulties, such as erection problems.

Some women are quite accepting of their partner's particular sexual preoccupations and may even happily participate in their sexual scenarios. However, a woman does have the right to her own sexual likes and dislikes, and she certainly has the right not to be pressured into going along with an activity that makes her uncomfortable or turns her off. As the pendulum has swung over recent decades from a conservative view of sexuality to more emphasis on experimentation and variety, I am seeing more women in Elizabeth's situation, where a man with an unusual sexual need takes the high moral ground and implies that the woman is inhibited or dysfunctional if she's not open to and accepting of his need. Her sexual needs and wants are often ignored, and sex becomes a trial for her, so it's not unreasonable that her libido would begin to decrease.

The Internet has led to new variations in paraphilias. Pornography has always been readily available, but now it's available at the click of a button. Although many people can use erotic material as a harmless aid to their sexual enjoyment, some people do get addicted to it, spending hours at a time on the Net, and this may lead to the need for the same type of scene in their sexual activity with their partner. Cybersex, in which people act out sexual activity with others they meet in chatrooms, is becoming more popular. It seems to me that men are more likely to get caught up in developing a need for this type of activity, but it can be powerful for some women as well. Cybersex can become a problem in a relationship either by taking the participant away from his relationship even though he is still at home or by creating sexual needs that he wants to play out with his partner. I have seen several cases in which the man has been visiting pornographic sites and then wants sex with his wife, whom he has ignored for several hours. The BDSM (bondage/discipline/sado-masochism) scene can have a particularly powerful influence, and I have seen couples in which the man wants his wife to become submissive to his dominant role, in which he directs every aspect of their sex life.

The issue with all these activities is not to cast judgment on them but to examine how they are played out in relationships. If both partners find pleasure and enjoyment in playing sexual games or using objects or clothing as aids during sex, there is no problem. And, as with any difference in sexual needs and wants, a woman may be willing to cooperate at times simply to please her partner. If she finds these things unacceptable, however, the couple has to deal with these differences with mutual respect. If one or both are unable to make changes so as to happily accommodate the other, it may mean that their best option is to end the relationship.

Relationship Problems

Kristy and Sean

The tension between Kristy and Sean was obvious as they walked into the room. Both had rigid expressions, and they sat stiffly in their chairs. Neither spoke.

"What can I do for you?" I asked.

After a brief silence, Kristy said angrily to Sean, "Well, aren't you going to say something? You're the one who's made a big deal out of this."

"If you call having to jump through hoops to get sex a big deal, then yes, I'm not happy with it." He turned to me. "She has this long list of things I have to do before she'll have sex. She gets cranky if I don't help with the kids or cook dinner or do the dishes, or if I'm late getting home, and then she uses that as an excuse not to have sex. She's always upset about something, but when I ask her what's wrong, she says, 'Nothing' or 'You should know.'"

"You don't do anything at home; I have to nag to get you to do anything," Kristy retorted. "Why should I have sex with you when you don't care about me?"

"So you're trying to punish me if you don't get your own way?" Sean asked. "It really burns me up that she can control sex, that she decides when we have it and when we don't."

"How can you expect me to even feel like sex when you're on my case all the time?" was Kristy's response.

"What other things do you argue about?" I asked.

"You name it, we argue about it," said Sean. "She spends money like I'm a millionaire and will not try to do a budget."

"He's a slob, and he expects me to pick up after him all the time," Kristy complained.

"There are a lot of things you each feel the other person does wrong, but what do you each feel your partner does right?" I asked.

There was only stony silence at that.

"You both seem to be able to let your partner know when you're angry; can you let your partner know when you're happy with him or her? How do you let each other know that you love each other, that you are pleased to see them, anything that lets your partner know what is right in the relationship?" I continued.

More silence.

Then Sean said angrily, "Isn't that what sex is supposed to do?"

Some therapists assume that significant relationship problems lie at the heart of most sexual problems, but, as I've said, I don't find this to be the case in most instances. It's certainly my experience that serious general relationship problems can disrupt sexual relationships, but the majority of couples in this situation recognize that their sexual problems are fallout from their other difficulties and don't categorize their concerns as primarily sexual. Many people in this situation are aware of their continuing desire for sex; they just don't want to have sex with their current partner.

Nevertheless, some couples come to therapy with their focus on sexual issues, and it doesn't take long for other problems to emerge. A good clue comes from the way the partners sit in the waiting room, walk into the consulting room, seat themselves in chairs, and talk about their problems. Kristy and Sean radiated hostility even before they began to speak. Sean was the one who organized the appointment because he was dissatisfied with their sex life. In his view, Kristy had the upper hand in their sexual relationship because, as he saw it, they had sex only when she wanted it, which he felt was unfair. He resented the fact that she would link other problems in their relationship to sex. When Kristy said that she did not feel like having sex because she was unhappy that he didn't help with the household chores or make an effort with the children, he felt that she made him "jump through hoops" just to get sex. Kristy was annoyed that she had to keep asking him to help her instead of having him help because he knew what had to be done, and when they did have sex, she was irritated that she had to keep telling him what she liked and didn't like. Sean was also angry about Kristy's poor financial management, and there were many other issues that led to conflict.

This couple split down the stereotypical gender lines. Kristy could not see how their sex life could improve unless their relationship improved, and Sean was adamant that if they had sex more often, he would be more willing to compromise with Kristy on other issues. This is a tricky situation for a therapist. How do you deal with the different points of view without seeming to side with one partner or the other? I agree that it's difficult for a woman to have sex and enjoy it if she is angry or resentful, so encouraging her to "just do it" in these circumstances will make the situation worse for her. Yet, from the man's perspective, he feels it's unreasonable to expect him to go for long periods without sex until all the relationship problems are sorted out.

My strategy is to try to shift the couple's focus to what is right between them. Why have they come to therapy to try to resolve their problems? What do they like about each other? If they can both identify good reasons to stay together and recognize aspects they like in each other, this is their motivation to listen to each other's point of view and try to find solutions rather than angrily state their individual positions and demand that the other partner do things their way. I ask each one, "What would you most like your partner to understand about how you feel? What is the most important thing your partner could do in the next few days that would help you feel he or she is concerned about you and trying to address the problems that are important to you? Then, what can you do in the next few days that would help your partner feel you really do care about him or her?"

By starting from this positive perspective, it's often possible for the couple to set in motion a positive cycle that encourages them to keep moving forward. Sean accepted that it was difficult for Kristy to feel like having sex when she was resentful, so he agreed that if Kristy let him know what she needed help with, he would do what he could. Kristy agreed to accept that Sean couldn't read her mind, to stop getting angry when he didn't always see what needed to be done, and to make an effort to express positive feelings with either affection or low-level sex rather than hold back. In general, over time, couples in strife have developed a pattern of communication in which they find it easy to express negative feelings but suppress anything positive, so the atmosphere of the relationship becomes increasingly poisoned. When this is combined with an absence of conflict-resolution skills, the relationship is in serious trouble. As many couples say, in the end they will argue about anything, even trivial issues.

Kristy and Sean had a lot of work to do before they could feel secure about the future of their relationship, but by combining relationship and sex therapy, they gradually made progress.

There are, however, some couples whose toxic relationship isn't salvageable. Ed and Margaret had a whirlwind romance and barely knew each other when they got married. It wasn't long after the wedding that they began to discover things about each other that they didn't like and couldn't agree on. Margaret's previously quiet existence was shattered by Ed's demanding and boisterous children, and her attempts to tame them proved frustrating to her and annoying to Ed. Ed believed that Margaret was tight with money; she thought he was too careless. Ed believed that Margaret had trapped him into marriage by pretending to be keen on sex; she felt her sex drive disappear as she tried to deal with the changes in her life and cope with Ed's sexual demands. Ed thought that Margaret was sexually inhibited because she wouldn't do the things he wanted, yet he was offended by her expectation that he should masturbate if he was sexually frustrated.

Ten months into the marriage, neither could identify any good reason to continue, although Ed was prepared to give it more time. Margaret wanted her old life back, could not see any possibility of the marriage giving her what she needed, and was relieved to call it quits.

Health and Medication

Debra and Jeremy

Debra was finding it difficult to get comfortable. I noticed that she had a slight limp when she walked into the room, but there was no plaster or crutches to give any clue as to what the cause might be.

"I was in a car accident three years ago," she explained. "The car rolled, and I was incredibly lucky. I came out with a broken arm, a broken leg, and some damage to my spine. The arm and leg got better, but my back still gives me some trouble. I can do most things I used to, although some things are difficult. And the reason I'm here is because my sex drive didn't come back."

Debra was in the hospital for two months after the accident, and she underwent months of physiotherapy to regain strength in her body and learn to do some things in new ways that didn't cause pain. About 12 months after the accident, she became depressed because she began to feel she would never get back to normal. With the love and support of her husband, Jeremy, and the use of antidepressants, she eventually got on top of things. She still took the medication because it helped with pain management and with periods where she got down about not being as active as she used to be.

"It's been hard to adjust to the different life. Oh, I know I'm lucky, I shouldn't complain, but I miss the sports I used to play,

and hiking and camping—and they are impossible now," she said. "I make myself do most of the housework, but if I do too much, I'm in a lot of pain the next day. I used to be on the go all the time, so it's really difficult to have to pace myself. I want to get back to normal, and I want to have the sex life we had. I want to want sex, I want to have fun, but when I think about sex, I think about the pain that can come suddenly if I move the wrong way. How do I get my sex drive back?"

Take a moment to think about your last bout of influenza, or when you had a toothache or a headache. How interested in sex were you then? Now imagine having the flu or the toothache or headache for weeks, months, or years without a break. This is similar to the situation in which some people who have a chronic illness or permanent disability find themselves. As much as they or their partner may wish it to be otherwise, the reality is that their sexual interest and enjoyment can be seriously compromised by lack of well-being, pain, and restricted mobility. On top of that, some of the medications used to control the health problems can decrease libido, inhibit arousal, and/or block orgasm.

The situation Debra found herself in after surviving a car accident is very common: Millions of Americans have chronic back injuries. The effect of such an injury on Debra's sexuality was threefold. First, there was the frustration that arose from the limitations the injuries imposed on her day-to-day life. She could no longer play the sports she used to, and she couldn't do many of the leisure activities she and Jeremy once enjoyed. Normal household chores were a major hassle; she could do most of them, but it took more time, and she was often sore the next day if she did too much. The realization that she would never return to her preinjury level of functioning meant that sometimes she felt down, although she hadn't had an episode of clinical depression for some time. Second, just as some ordinary activities were restricted because they were painful, Debra found that some sexual techniques and positions were no longer pleasurable or possible because they hurt. If she was already sore because of the things she had done during the day, she was unlikely to be too enthusiastic about sex, and even if she didn't start out in pain, moving the wrong way could lead to discomfort, so she lost arousal and enjoyment. The third way her injury affected her sex life was connected with the medications she took to ease her depression and control her pain. All of these effects combined to significantly reduce her libido, and she missed the sexual person she used to be.

There are many other chronic conditions that have similar effects on sexual function. Arthritis, migraines, kidney failure, and heart conditions are just a few. The challenge for the couple is to shift their focus from what they have lost to what is still possible and to maximize the pleasure of sex by moving into relationship sex mode. Some people I see have a hard time accepting this, which is understandable, but it may be the only way they can maintain their sexual relationship.

Some physical problems are specific to women. Melanie, whom we met earlier in this chapter, suffered a serious tear in her vagina during childbirth that caused painful scarring. Even after an attempt to repair the damage, she found intercourse uncomfortable because of the scar tissue and adhesions, and this had the effect of dampening her libido and causing her to avoid intercourse. Her husband tried to be supportive and understanding, but he couldn't help feeling that if he stayed with Melanie, it seemed unlikely that he would ever have a normal sex life. This couple had many difficult issues to address before they were able to deal with the changes to their sex life, but with mutual love and support they came to terms with it.

It can be difficult for men to understand what it feels like to have a penis thrusting into a tender vagina, and some men certainly give their partner the impression that they believe it can't possibly be that bad and they should just get on with it. Some women have recurring episodes of yeast infections and during these times should avoid intercourse, but I see women who feel guilty about depriving their partner. The attitude that her partner's pleasure is more important than her own discomfort is disturbing and suggests that we still have a long way to go in putting the importance of sex in perspective. It also fails to acknowledge that the woman may also be feeling sad or frustrated by the absence of sex.

Take Ellen and Tom, for example. Ellen had recurring episodes of thrush over more than a year and wisely avoided intercourse at those times. Ellen was a woman who under normal circumstances had a strong sex drive and relied on penile thrusting to achieve orgasm. She was seriously annoyed by the reaction of friends to their plight when they were discussing sexual matters at a dinner party: The response of the men and even some of the women was "Poor Tom!"

Endometriosis can also lead to painful intercourse. This condition occurs when tissue similar to the lining of the womb is found on organs outside it, creating sticky masses that can cause adhesions. This means that organs become stuck together at various points, whereas in a healthy woman, they slide past each other as she moves her body. For a woman with endometriosis, bending and twisting during normal daily activities, including intercourse, makes the adhesions pull on the organs and cause pain. Typically, the pain occurs with deep thrusting, but as the woman becomes anxious about the possibility of pain during intercourse, she tends to tense the pelvic floor muscles that contain the vagina, which makes it difficult for the penis to enter and causes pain at the mouth of the vagina. Thankfully, not all women with endometriosis have these problems, but those who do can find their sex life severely affected. Some women respond to the available treatments, but others don't.

Another vaginal problem that is very frustrating for the woman, her partner, and her medical practitioner is burning vulva syndrome, also known as vestibulitis and vulvodynia. It's characterized by burning or stinging pain on penetration and during thrusting. Typically, the woman has a burning, red, and sometimes swollen vaginal opening for some hours after intercourse, and she may find that urination causes stinging. It's only been within the past decade or so that this problem has been taken seriously by medical practitioners; prior to that, these symptoms were assumed to be entirely psychological in origin and to arise from fear or inhibition about sex.

Though it's now recognized that there must be a physical cause or causes for this problem, researchers have a long way to go in identifying what they may be, although there are quite a few theories. And because the cause has not been established, there is no reliable treatment protocol. Various treatment strategies seem to help some women, but they are discovered only by trial and error. This situation is a good example of the caution that health professionals must exercise before telling a woman her problems are all in her head; rather, they should admit that they don't have enough information to adequately diagnose and treat the problem.

In the past, women who experienced loss of sexual sensation after a hysterectomy were also routinely told that they were suffering from a psychological reaction to the loss of their womb and, by inference, their womanhood, so that psychologically they could no longer allow themselves to respond sexually as women. In 1998, an Australian urological surgeon, Dr. Helen O'Connell, conducted autopsies on several female cadavers and made some startling discoveries when she removed the clitorises. She found that the clitoris is much larger and the neural network that feeds it and sends signals back to the brain is much more extensive and complex than was previously acknowledged. This means that some types of pelvic surgery, such as hysterectomy, could cause damage to the clitoral neural pathways, resulting in major loss of sensation. It seems that women who experience loss of sexual pleasure after a hysterectomy are not neurotic after all.

The sad news for women who have chronic medical problems is that there may not be any treatment that will lead to significant improvement in sexual function. Medical science will never be able to treat all conditions and produce perfect outcomes, including problems affecting sexual function. Thus, a couple in this situation has some difficult issues to solve together because it may be that their sex life will always be limited by the woman's condition, either in terms of her low interest in sex or the physical activities they can pursue. A strong and loving relationship can help them build on the sensual and emotional aspects of their limited sexual activity.

There is also still much to be done in understanding the impact of medications on sexual function, although we have come a long way from the time I first trained as a sex therapist in the early 1970s. At that time, there was a lot of denial among health professionals and pharmaceutical companies about the sexual side effects of prescribed drugs. Despite the high doses of hormones being pumped into women with the early oral contraceptives, for example, if a woman complained of loss of libido, she was told that the problem lay with her, not the Pill. Men taking medications for high blood pressure were told a similar story if they experienced problems with erections. Now almost any drug is suspect, as hundreds of medications have known effects on sexual function. They cause a loss of function in two ways: directly, such as the inhibition of ejaculation and orgasm that occurs with some antidepressants, or indirectly, such as the nausea that can be associated with some anti-inflammatory medication or fatigue that's a side effect of tranquilizers. In the same way, recreational drugs, such as alcohol, marijuana, heroin, cocaine, and so on can cause sexual impairment.

LIVING IN A LESS-THAN-PERFECT WORLD

I recently read that one sex therapist's solution to low libido was to look at all the things that were dampening a person's sex drive and eliminate them. In a perfect world, that should be possible, but few of us are so fortunate as to be able to banish from our life everything that gets us down. All of the issues we have explored in this chapter are real problems that happen to real, normal people, so it's perfectly normal and reasonable that people struggle to maintain their sex life, particularly if they believe they should be performing according to the current standards of good sex. I developed the concept of relationship sex to help not only those who were naturally at the more quiet end of the sexuality range but also those who might, under better circumstances, be more energetic and passionate but for whom life was throwing up challenges that made this unlikely.

The idea of relationship sex is really nothing new. I find there are many couples living through trying circumstances who have adjusted their sex life to suit, although they may worry that there is something wrong with them because they accept their new sexual situation and may even be content. Should they try harder? they wonder; are they letting their partner down? I am most impressed by these couples, who may need only reassurance that they really are doing the best they can and that their main task is to trust themselves and their relationship to find their own solutions.

In a less-than-perfect world, there are often less-than-perfect solutions, but if a couple works together, they can find answers that are good enough. Sometimes, these answers aren't obvious, and the couple finds it difficult to work through the issues on their own. Some sort of map is needed to help point them in the right direction to reach their sexual potential, whatever their circumstances, and that is what I explore in the next section.

Building Your Intimate Relationship

CHAPTER 8

WORKING TOGETHER ON YOUR SEXUAL RELATIONSHIP

USUALLY, WHEN A WOMAN CONSULTS ME ABOUT HER LOW LIBIDO, she hopes that I will have a treatment program that will reveal the secrets of hot desire and great sex and show her how to break through her personal inhibitions so she can reach out and grab this prize. Some women believe this will require prolonged therapy, and others tell me at their first appointment that their partner is at home expecting great things that evening.

I feel as if I am bursting some bubbles when I explain my ideas about normal sexuality and admit that I don't know of any treatment strategy that will guarantee the sex life my clients are hoping for. Yet, as the initial session progresses, the most common reaction I get is profound relief: "You mean I'm not strange after all?"

For some couples, this relief is enough to help them turn their attention to what they are already doing that is enjoyable and satisfying. By talking more confidently with each other, they are reassured that they're not letting each other down, and although they may be a little disappointed if this is as good as it gets, they are happy. These are the couples who come back for their next sessions to report that while nothing much has changed in what they are doing, they feel much better, and they believe they can work things out for themselves from that point.

Other couples are tangled in the anti-libido cycle and need more assistance to work their way through the particular issues that are limiting their sexual potential and causing them such distress. What I have tried to do is develop an approach that offers a win-win outcome. It is based on several assumptions.

- Individual differences exist.
- Gender differences exist.
- No sex therapy program can make someone become someone they are not.
- Good sex is more than doing the right behaviors.
- Love can be expressed in many different ways in a sexual relationship.
- Sex has many different functions in a long-term relationship.
- Sex drive will not increase through argument or emotional pressure.

The last point is critical to my approach: I have never seen a woman's libido increase as a result of argument, criticism, or conflict—in fact, just the reverse happens. My approach works best if you are respectful of each other, you are both prepared to change, and you are genuinely interested in discovering what your partner wants and needs in order to improve sexual desire and enjoyment, even if it is different from what you would like. Sometimes, an unexpected positive outcome is that by taking the pressure off the woman and developing her confidence to trust her own judgment about what is right for her sexually, she finds her physical interest in sex improves, and she experiences the hot feelings she was hoping for. Even if this doesn't happen, if you are each prepared to be confidently and generously involved in the give-and-take process, sex will become desirable for both of you because it meets so many emotional and sensual needs. The end result is that you'll both feel valued, appreciated, and loved.

BEFORE YOU BEGIN

If the anti-libido cycle has been operating in your relationship for some time, it may be hard to feel motivated to change if you are overwhelmed

CLASSIFYING SEXUAL PROBLEMS

Sex therapists classify sexual problems as either lifelong or acquired. Lifelong problems are cases in which the person with the troubling behavior has always performed that way, and acquired problems are those that have developed after a period of performing at a more acceptable level. Thus, some women have never, under any circumstances, been able to come to orgasm (lifelong), while some have done so at some stage in their life and now for some reason are unable to (acquired). Some men have always had rapid ejaculatory response with all partners (lifelong), while some have had periods of longer response time but now tend to ejaculate soon after penetration on most occasions (acquired).

In general, lifelong problems are more likely to be just the way a particular person is, although there is always the possibility that the person's sexual potential has been limited from the start by poor sex education or a preexisting psychological problem, such as a history of abuse. Acquired problems indicate that something has happened during the course of a person's sex life to disrupt what was until that time the normal level of sexual functioning. This disruption could be something like a brief period of stress or a prolonged situation such as chronic illness. Acquired problems are more likely to respond to sex therapy than lifelong ones are, but this is not black and white, and what complicates the situation greatly is that it's extremely difficult to predict which people in either group are likely to benefit and which aren't.

by feelings of hurt, rejection, or anger. The process of change can begin only when you have been able to talk to each other about why you want the relationship to continue and what you still mean to each other. The first step is to take some time to think about why you want to stay in your relationship.

There are many reasons that you might choose to stay with your partner. Of course, there are couples who come to realize that their relationship has a lot going for it, but they just lost sight of these things for a while. Some people say they are staying because of the children, and others cite financial or emotional security. Women in particular worry whether they are staying for the "right" reasons. These worries are fueled by popular advice, such as it's wrong to stay together just for the children. There also seems to be a general belief that the only genuine reason to stay in a relationship is if you are "in love" with your partner—that merely loving or caring for him is not enough. *Love* is such an overworked word, distorted by images presented to us daily in the media, that it has almost no meaning. Questions like, Surely, if I love him, wouldn't I want to have sex with him? (i.e., feel turned on by his touch) confuse the picture as to what love is all about.

Ask yourself, Is there enough between us to give this a chance? and Do I want to solve this problem, or do I only want to make a token effort and sabotage everything we try, just to make it look as if I've given it a chance? Rather than trying to pin down "love," ask, Do I care about this person? and What will I lose if this relationship ends? The most basic question to consider is, Will my life be better if we're together or apart? After all, separation doesn't necessarily bring a better, happier life.

Sometimes, if your relationship has been in strife for a while, you may be faced with two difficult choices. Separation and divorce are not easy, but if you stay, there are no guarantees that the problems will resolve. It makes sense to stay together only if you *both* want to work to build your relationship. Do you feel that you are both striving for the same thing—a loving relationship? Sex shouldn't be something that comes between you; surely you are both on the same team, on the same side. Neither one of you is right or wrong, and sexual difficulties can be resolved only if you can encourage and support each other over the coming months. If either of you does genuinely believe that one partner is deliberately intending to hurt the other, there isn't much point in focusing on your sexual issues since there are clearly more serious matters to address.

Before we go any further, each partner should consider some basic questions about their situation.

The man with the higher drive sometimes asks, "What about my sexual wants and needs? What happens if she never wants sex as often as I do, never wants to do the things I'd like? Why should I have to miss out?"

I would reply, "Why is it so important to you? Is it more important than other aspects of your relationship?" There are many things in life that we may want but never get—more money, a better job, a more comfortable home. Are you going to dwell on what you don't have, or make the most of what is within reach? Your partner is not responsible for your sexual needs, and it is just as reasonable for her to expect you to modify your sexual expectations as it is for you to ask her to increase sexual activity. It may help if you can identify what you miss most about not having sex as often as you'd like and explore whether this need can be met in some other way. For example, many men say it's not the lack of sexual release that distresses them but rather the lack of emotional closeness. In these cases, it's often possible for the couple to increase general affection that does not always lead to sex. If physical sexual frustration is the problem, alternatives such as masturbation can be a solution.

The woman with low drive may ask, "Why should I have to have sex at all? If I don't feel like it, why can't we just live without it?" I certainly don't believe you should *have* to have sex, but it is a normal, healthy part of a caring relationship. It's your right to choose to live a celibate life, but your partner isn't being unreasonable if this isn't what he wants. You can't, however, increase your sexual desire simply to please your partner or save your marriage. For any improvement to be meaningful and to last, you can seek only to develop your sexuality for yourself. It feels good to want sex, to enjoy it, to be aroused and have an orgasm, at least sometimes. At the moment, you are focusing on what you have to give to your partner to satisfy him, and that can be a real turnoff. You have to find out what you can get from sex and what makes it good for you, even if this is different from what your partner expects. Only by understanding your own sexuality and being assertive about your wants and needs will you begin to want sex more often.

Third-Party Involvement

No sex therapy program is likely to help you improve your sexual relationship with your partner if you are currently involved with someone else. Clearly, the issues between you and your partner have escalated to a critical stage, you are at a crossroads, and you are faced with a difficult decision. If your relationship with your partner has broken down to the extent that you can't see a good future with him, then you are already emotionally detaching from him, and it can be very difficult to re-establish any level of sexual desire.

However, if you feel you still love your partner, but sex is more exciting with your lover, you may need to do a reality check. It's not surprising that having an affair leads to more erotic sex, because all the things that help a woman turn on are an integral part of the situation. You and your lover spend time together that is usually focused exclusively on each other, there is plenty of sensuous affectionate touch as well as deeply intimate discussions, emotions are heightened because of the secrecy surrounding your relationship, sexual tension builds as you anticipate the next meeting, and you have usually set aside time to devote to sex. This is similar to the infatuation stage of any relationship—the stage in which women are more likely to be aware of physical passion. Day-to-day living with your long-term partner usually doesn't offer the same intensity of emotion and sexual feeling.

To be fair to your partner and to yourself, you need to decide

TESTOSTERONE REPLACEMENT THERAPY

Of all the issues that a sex therapist is asked to deal with, libido problems are the most complex. The latest treatment for female low libido is testosterone replacement therapy (TRT), but it's wise to be cautious about what it can offer. The best available research is on menopausal women; it appears to be beneficial for about 50 percent of those complaining of loss of libido. Research on premenopausal women is still in its early stages, and there are many questions yet to be answered. There's still no reliable data on normal levels of testosterone in young women, so we really don't know what constitutes testosterone deficiency. If TRT does increase a woman's libido, how long would she need to remain on it? My guess is that if the woman's current level of libido is what is normal for her, then any benefits of TRT will occur only while she takes it. The effects of long-term use of TRT are unknown, although some side effects have been identified.

My concern with TRT is that it's likely to become the equivalent of diet pills in the weight-control industry. Certainly there are women who need medical help to reduce their weight, and they do well on the drugs, with the benefits outweighing any disadvantages. But diet pills are also used by women who are trying to conform to an artificial standard of desirable weight. Often, women set goal weights below what is healthy for them, and the only way they can stay at those weights is to continue taking the pills. In addition, the use of diet pills as a first line of treatment means that other factors are not addressed—so again, once she stops taking the pills, any weight loss will be reversed. The possible parallels with TRT as a first-line treatment for complaints of low libido are obvious, particularly as long as sex drive is defined only as a physical desire for sex and we expect women to behave in a particular way to demonstrate that they have "normal" sex drive.

whether what is right in that relationship means enough to you that you can end your affair and appreciate the possibilities in your sexual relationship with your partner, given that it's unlikely to develop the same levels of excitement and passion you have with your lover.

I must point out, however, that most women with low libido find it difficult to generate enough energy to have sex with their husband, let alone with anyone else. It is, of course, a doubt that crosses the minds of many men: "If she doesn't want sex with me, she must be getting it somewhere else." If your partner raises this issue with you, you can only reassure him that this is not the case.

A Word of Caution

If you feel distressed, angry, or resentful during sex, I suggest that you take time to explore these emotions before you proceed. These feelings may arise because of past experiences with sex, such as sexual abuse; because you feel emotionally manipulated into having sex by your partner; or because, even if your partner isn't pressuring you in any way, your own guilt leads you to say yes when you really want to say no. Whatever the reason, continuing to have sex under these circumstances is likely to harm your future healthy sexual adjustment. Instead of experiencing sex in a positive, happy way, you associate it with negative, destructive feelings.

Take some time to sit quietly on your own with a pen and paper. Write, "When I'm having sex, I feel upset (or angry or resentful) because . . ." Write down anything that comes to mind. You may need to try this on several occasions over a couple of weeks before you get to what is bothering you. When you have some idea what the issues are, you'll be in a better position to decide what to do about them.

You may be able to resolve your feelings by discussing their causes with your partner, particularly if his behavior is the trigger for your distress. However, you may need to see a marriage counselor or sex therapist together or visit a therapist on your own before you decide what to do about any other sexual issues.

USING MY APPROACH

Because circumstances vary from couple to couple, the approach outlined in the following chapters can be adapted to suit your requirements. As you read through each chapter, use what information seems to apply to you and ignore any that isn't relevant. However, if one of you thinks a section is relevant and the other doesn't, you need to have a discussion about this difference in point of view before you move on. To get the most out of this approach, I suggest you have a notebook and pen handy to jot down notes and ideas to help you organize your thoughts and to focus on the issues you want to share with your partner.

CHAPTER 9

EXPLORING YOUR SEXUAL POTENTIAL

YOU ARE READING THIS BOOK BECAUSE YOU'RE CONCERNED about your lack of interest in sex and its impact on your relationship. You'd very much like to improve this situation, but the usual advice to dress up in sexy clothing or try different techniques and positions to help you get into a passionate, erotic mood does nothing to help you want sex more often. My approach is to recognize that although everyone has the capacity to be a sensual, emotional, sexual person, the reality is that this means different things to different people. Now we have to figure out what will help you feel more interested in participating in sex, get more out of sex, and enhance your intimate relationship.

THE SEXUAL YOU

Throughout the preceding chapters, I have frequently made the point that the definition of sex drive as a strong sense of physical urgency for sex is too narrow and that many women never or rarely experience this type of sexual desire.

I don't disagree that it would be lovely to have that physical desire for sex, and I'm sure it would make you and your partner feel great if you sometimes looked at him and felt almost desperate to have sex with him, but suppose that despite your best efforts, it doesn't happen. Does that mean you give up on your sex life?

What I am asking you to do is to try to become aware of other reasons to want sex, not just a feeling of physical desire. This is where your relationship with your partner comes in. Can you want sex because this is the man you love, and you want to be close and intimate with him? Can you want sex because life has been dumping on you, and you would like some comfort and reassurance? Can you want sex because, although you're not aware of feeling at all aroused at the moment, you know you can turn on once you get started, and an orgasm would be nice?

What this means is that you need to decide that you want sex because of what you're going to get from it. As the anti-libido cycle has kicked in for you over recent months or years, sex has become a real hassle. Research tells us that many women choose to have sex to please their partner, and this is not necessarily a bad thing, but if you feel that you've had to focus on what you have to give your partner to keep the peace or to stop him from feeling hurt or rejected, there has probably been very little pleasure in it for you.

If you groan inwardly and think, "Oh, no, I can't be bothered," when you know he wants sex, or you stay up late to avoid it, this tells me you are thinking about sex in terms of what you have to give, not what you can get. Unfortunately, this attitude gets in the way of being aware of and appreciating whatever nice feelings might be there for you. We need to uncover any positive feelings at all that will help you feel okay about having sex—the beginning of discovering your sex drive.

Work Out What Makes Sex More Appealing

"Do you ever feel like having sex?" I am sometimes surprised by the answer when I ask this question of women who worry that they have an

A TYPICAL COUPLE: DEBBIE AND ALAN

Debbie and Alan were chatting in the waiting room when I came to call them in for their consultation. Alan took Debbie's hand as they followed me into the consulting room. When they were settled, I asked how I could help them. Debbie looked at Alan, who gave an encouraging smile, and she began to talk about her lack of interest in sex. Both in their late thirties, the couple had two children, a 10-year-old girl and an 8-year-old boy. They were financially comfortable. Alan had a job as a computer programmer, which he enjoyed. Debbie worked three days a week as a lawyer, and found this a good balance between her career needs and having the time with the kids that she felt was important.

"I just can't be bothered having sex, and it's really worrying me," Debbie began. "Sex was really good for the first couple of years, but it's now at the stage where if Alan didn't make the first move, it would never happen, and often when he does start something, I tell him no. We made the appointment because we had a long talk about it recently, but that didn't solve anything, and we both ended up quite upset."

Alan joined in. "I told her I wasn't going to make the first move any more; I was going to leave it up to her. I hate the feeling that I am pressuring her into doing something she doesn't want to do, and yet if she does turn me down, I feel hurt. Sometimes when we are having sex, she seems to relax and enjoy it, but other

abnormally low libido. The answers they give range from "a couple of times a week" to "never!" Do all of these women have low libidos?

I saw an interesting case a few years ago that highlights the fact that libido problems are relevant only in the context of specific relationships. The times she doesn't seem to be there at all, and then I feel like I'm just using her. But I know from past experience that if I do leave it up to her, weeks can go by and we don't have sex. I just want her to want sex and to enjoy it."

"Alan has been wonderful," Debbie said. "I'm sure other men would have left by now. He really tries hard to find out what would help, he asks me what I want him to do, and he'll take as much time as I need to get aroused. Nothing has helped, and it's getting worse rather than better. Now I don't like him touching me at all, even if he wants to cuddle while we're watching television. I get tense and worry whether it will lead to sex."

"It's actually the lack of affection that bothers me the most," explained Alan. "I start to think that it must be me, that maybe she has stopped loving me, or I'm no longer sexually attractive to her, or maybe I'm just a bad lover."

As the couple kept talking, checking with each other for reassurance, both taking care not to be hurtful to the other, a familiar picture emerged. Debbie and Alan were typical of many of the couples I see whose relationships are basically sound: Each was doing the best they could to be considerate of the other, yet both were worried that her take-it-or-leave-it attitude about sex meant that something was terribly wrong somewhere, and they had no idea what to do about it.

husband had a demanding job that involved an hour of commuting each way, so he was quite tired on weekday evenings. He had the energy for sex only on weekends, which his wife interpreted as indicating there was something wrong with him, because she wanted sex two or three times a week.

I saw the couple for a few sessions, but it was already too late, and they divorced. About three years later, the same woman came to see me with her second husband, and this time she was the one in the hot seat. He wanted sex at least once a day, and she just couldn't keep up. They managed to work things out, although he wasn't happy about having to compromise.

This example illustrates why problems arising from differences in libido have to be dealt with by both partners. This is obviously easier for a woman who knows that she does have a sex drive, even if it's not as strong as her partner's. She can feel more confident about tackling the libido difference on a more equal basis, with the understanding that although she and her partner have different levels of sex drive, they are both normal.

If you feel you could easily live without sex, however, we need to start with the basic questions. Are there at least some occasions when the idea of sex is appealing? If so, try to figure out what makes the difference. Are you more interested at certain times of the month or when you're on vacation or at a certain time of the day? Sometimes, the circumstances under which your partner expects you to have sex may be part of the problem. Consider the case of Stan and Faye, whom we met in chapter 7. Stan could not understand why his wife, Faye, wasn't keen for sex if he woke her when he got home from work in the early hours of the morning. Some couples simply have different biological clocks: Maybe the woman prefers sex at night and her husband prefers it in the morning, but she's the one who is identified as having low libido because she won't suggest sex if she knows he isn't in the mood, whereas he can be quite persistent until she finally gives in.

If you can't figure out what helps you get interested, can you work out what definitely turns you off? The turnoffs that women talk to me about include foreplay being either too abrupt and clumsy or too long and involved, intercourse being too quick or lasting too long , and the entire session being too brief or too prolonged. Knowing that a particular technique such as oral or anal sex is always expected or that your partner will never be happy with whatever happens are also turnoffs.

I know that for some women, a turnoff can be something basic, such as their partner's poor personal hygiene or bad breath. If this is the case for you, are you reluctant to raise the issue because you don't want to offend your partner?

Once you have identified what helps you get interested or what turns you off, you need to explain this clearly and confidently to your partner. No matter how trivial the issue seems or whether you hate something that every other woman apparently thoroughly enjoys, if it's relevant to your low libido, it needs to be taken seriously. If your partner refuses to listen to you and accuses you of just making excuses to avoid sex, it may be time to visit a relationship counselor.

Sometimes, though, the bottom line is that while you love your husband, who may be very caring and considerate, you really don't feel like sex, which seems like merely another chore to do. Debbie and Alan (see page 136) have a sound relationship, yet Debbie says that often sex just seems like too much hassle.

The couples who consult me about the woman's low libido can be any age and may have been together for a few years or a couple of decades. They probably have the usual life stresses—busy lives filled with children, work, domestic chores, and friends. The partners regard each other as best friends, they can discuss most problems without any heat, they rarely argue seriously, and they find it easy to be loving and considerate toward each other. They usually nominate their worry about their sex life as the only serious issue of concern in their relationship.

Like Debbie, the woman describes the sexual difficulties the couple is experiencing as being her fault, but even if he doesn't openly say it as Alan did, the man worries that somehow he is the real problem. The woman reports that she often feels irritation at being fondled on the breasts or genitals and is rarely aware of any physical desire or lustiness. If she does sometimes feel at all lusty, either her partner isn't around and the feelings are gone by the time he's available, or she doesn't act on the feelings because she thinks her partner will expect her to be really hot, and she isn't confident she can be that way. She may also avoid affection because she's worried it will lead to sex.

Mostly, it just never occurs to her to initiate sex, and her reaction when her partner does is to think, "I can't be bothered." She finds she is easily distracted during sexual activity, and because it may be hard work to come to orgasm when she's tired, she prefers not to even try. She may make the decision to have sex based on a willingness to please her partner, and she sometimes regrets it and wants it all to end quickly. Foreplay may be annoying despite her partner's best efforts to please her, and prolonged intercourse is usually boring. Yet, for a surprising number of couples, confusion arises because there are times when, despite initial lack of interest, she responds with passion. Why doesn't this happen every time, and if she can enjoy sex, why doesn't she ever seem to want it?

Later, we'll get to suggestions to try during lovemaking that may help you enjoy it more, but the major difficulty you are having is making the initial decision to have sex. Sometimes, instead of waiting to *feel* like having sex, you can try to *think* yourself into doing it. Some sex therapists tell women to "just do it," but I find that often this can feel like just another pressure, and the decision to have sex needs to feel a bit more reasonable and positive. I've had discussions with many women about how they talk themselves into having sex. For example, one woman felt that sex once a week was reasonable, so she would think something like, "Hmm, we've been a little distant lately, and he is such a sweetheart. It would be nice to feel close again—and tonight's a better night because the kids have gone to bed early, and we don't have to get up early tomorrow. So, yes, I think sex is okay."

All right, I agree, this isn't very romantic, and it certainly isn't what we think sex drive should be, but it is a beginning. In the next chapter, we'll explore a range of triggers that may help you find it easier to say yes to sex more often.

Identify What Has Helped in the Past

Some women can recall periods earlier in their lives when they actually did feel like having sex. Debbie was typical of the majority of women in this category; she used to feel more like having sex in the early years of their relationship, but then her life became somewhat more hectic as she juggled work, children, and home. Alan adored her, was helpful with the kids and the chores, and was a considerate lover, so her low libido was not about a poor relationship. Rather, her change in libido was a reflection of who she was at that time in her life. As we explored all the things that might make it easier for Debbie to be interested in sex, she realized that before she had children, she would take time in the evenings to unwind by herself, and she really missed that. She and Alan decided that they would designate the half hour after the children went to bed as Debbie's time, even if she spent that time staring into space. Then she felt she had more energy to focus on their relationship.

If you were more interested in sex in the past, can you recall some of the things that helped you feel that way at that time in your life? If you and your partner used to spend more time together, is there any way you can get a break away from the kids? Do you need more nonsexual affection? More gentle foreplay? Did your partner once spend more time on playful or relaxing foreplay, such as tickling your neck or having a chat over a cup of coffee or a glass of wine, than he does now?

Rather than trying to pinpoint reasons for a general unraveling of your sex life, perhaps you can identify specific issues that occurred at the time of your loss of sexual desire. Kathy, who we met in an earlier chapter, found her interest in sex waning when her partner, Gary, made sex very stressful for her because he believed she wasn't having orgasms. Similarly, Elizabeth was turned off by Martin's need to sit and look at her vulva as part of foreplay, and Matthew made sex painful and boring for Jenny because he took too long to come during intercourse. In cases such as these, the cooperation of the woman's partner is essential if her libido is to recover. Both Gary and Matthew were quite prepared to address their contributions to the problem, so Kathy and Jenny found that their libido slowly increased. Martin wouldn't accept that his behavior was the reason that Elizabeth didn't want sex, and their relationship ultimately collapsed.

If you ask yourself, What was happening in my life when my libido started to lessen? and you realize that it started when you were dealing with a serious issue or life event, be patient and look after yourself, and in time, your libido may slowly recover. In the meantime, gentle and comforting relationship sex can soothe you and maintain your sexual relationship with your partner.

Explore Your Ability to Have Orgasms

We have seen that women vary greatly in their ability to climax. To the great envy of others, some women have no difficulty reaching orgasm whenever they have sex. Despite the fact that an orgasm with penile thrusting is difficult for lots of women, some do find that it happens easily for them.

Certainly the ability to have an orgasm by any means at all can help a woman feel somewhat keener to have sex. Sometimes, although you don't consciously feel aroused or interested, you can decide that an orgasm would be good and readily respond to your partner's advances. This approach depends on your confidence that you can have an orgasm if you feel like having one. The strategies for helping women improve orgasmic response have remained much the same for the past several decades, so if you'd like to explore this further, there are many books that may help (see Recommended Reading on page 213 for more information).

However, being able to have an orgasm is no guarantee that you will experience a desire for sex on a regular, consistent basis. This is the difference between sex drive and sexual response. While some women certainly are aware of sexual frustration if they don't have regular orgasms, even for many easily orgasmic women, the thought of sex still just doesn't cross their mind, and they aren't aware of a need to have an orgasm. This is a source of great frustration to a partner: If he can get her to agree to have sex, she can usually get aroused and climax, so why on earth doesn't she want it?

The answer isn't straightforward, and it may be different for different women. One woman may simply think that orgasm isn't such a big deal. Sure, maybe she can have good orgasms, but so what? There are lots of other nice feelings that may be just as important to her or that she may enjoy even more. This attitude seems unbelievable in today's society, where sex has been elevated to almost religious status. But who is to say how often someone should want orgasm or how important it should be? Particularly if a woman is tired, trying to have an orgasm can be hard work, and even if she gets there, it may not seem worth the effort. Feeling pressured to have an orgasm when it just isn't a priority can be a good reason for a woman to avoid sex.

The same line of thinking applies to women who know they can't reach orgasm at all if they are tired or preoccupied. This is what was happening with Debbie. She realized that she had to be in the right mood to get there, so if she wasn't, she'd say no to sex. Debbie and Alan were both happy to find that her desire for quiet and cuddly sex at times was quite normal, and the freedom not to have orgasm every time was a great boost to her interest in sex.

I've said previously that no sex therapy program will suit everyone, and there are women who don't like the concept of relationship sex. They just don't see the point of sex unless they can be aroused and come to orgasm like their partner. If this is the case for you, the best solution is to make sex more of a priority and give it the time you need to make orgasm achievable. It's also worth exploring training programs that may make it easier for you to come when you're tired, perhaps by using a vibrator/massager or self-stimulation. However, a few women want ideal sex and believe it should be possible to feel a strong sex drive and have orgasm easily with intercourse no matter what, so they can't accept alternatives such as masturbation. I don't have a program that can guarantee that outcome, so, given their current life circumstances, their frequency of sex will remain dependent on opportunities for erotic sex as they arise.

Sometimes, an orgasmic woman avoids sex because of the way she comes to orgasm. She may require a lot of stimulation, maybe 10 minutes or longer of manual or oral attention, before she even comes close. She worries that her partner is bored or that his hand or jaw is aching, and this means she takes even longer. Maybe she can come only if she is touched in a certain way, and either her partner has trouble doing it right, or she is too embarrassed to tell him every time what she needs. The simplest solution is for her to learn how to bring herself to orgasm with masturbation, either with a vibrator/massager or by hand, and use this method during sex with her partner.

Self-stimulation is usually a lot quicker and more efficient than partner stimulation, so when the partner's efforts take a long time, incorporating self-stimulation makes sense. However, this is embarrassing for some women, and some men feel offended if they're not successful in helping their partner climax. Certainly a lot of women who stimulate themselves during sexual activity don't want their partner to watch. Generally, I suggest that the man do other things while she touches her genitals, such as cuddling, stroking, massaging, or engaging in intercourse, so that both partners feel that it's a shared activity.

In contrast to the woman who finds it difficult to have an orgasm unless conditions are right for her, there is the largely unrecognized concern of some women who feel they climax too quickly. Two large surveys, one in the United States and one in Australia, found that about 10 percent of women reported that they came too soon. Worry about early orgasm is usually thought to be a male problem, and indeed, it is the major sexual anxiety of men, with about one in three believing they ejaculate too rapidly. With the few women I have seen who feel they come too quickly, either they climax almost as soon as penetration occurs, or they come to orgasm after a few minutes of penile thrusting, while their partner lasts much longer. In both situations, the women find continued stimulation irritating once they have climaxed. Although some women are multiorgasmic, many are not, and after one orgasm, a woman may be too physically sensitive to be able to tolerate further stimulation. Again, if this is your problem, you need to address it with your partner. The most useful strategy is probably to spend more time on sensual rather than intensely sexual foreplay for you, with more direct stimulation of the penis prior to penetration for him.

If you can come to orgasm only through an unusual method, perhaps by rubbing against an object, such as a chair, or pulling something, such as the sheets, between your legs, or only when you are lying in specific positions, there are orgasmic retraining strategies to help you respond more easily to a wider range of stimulation. These strategies start with the means you're accustomed to and over weeks and months introduce gradual changes to the type of stimulation you would receive with your partner. So, if you have always masturbated lying on your stomach, and now that's the only way you can come, you would continue to practice masturbation regularly, gradually altering your position so that over time, you learn to be orgasmic in different positions.

These options to improve your orgasmic ability are worth exploring because deciding that an orgasm would be nice can sometimes help motivate you to have sex.

Appreciate Your Body

What do you think when you see yourself naked in the mirror? Research tells us that about 80 percent of young women are unhappy with the way they look—80 percent! I see so many young, attractive women who tell me they are fat and ugly, or their hair isn't right, or their buttocks or thighs are too wide. Even genuine reassurance from their partner that they look great to them seems to do little to make these women feel better.

Older women also have problems with body image, and some seriously doubt that their husband can find them at all sexually attractive. In my doctoral research project on postnatal loss of sexual desire and enjoyment, I found that the majority of new mothers felt they were more unattractive than before their pregnancy, and this was related to their loss of desire.

A lot of women I talk to can't relax and enjoy sex because they are aware of their body. Do you avoid letting your partner see you naked? Do you avoid playing sexual games because you're worried you don't look the part? Maybe, after childbirth, your tummy does seem to be a bit flabby and bounce around independently when you move during sex, or as you get older, your breasts aren't as firm as they used to be. Just because you feel unattractive, however, that doesn't mean that your partner sees you that way. I am worried by how many women can't accept the fact that a man might see them as a whole person and be turned on by who they are, including the less-than-perfect figure.

Actually, I think it's rather insulting to your partner, who can recognize that there is more to a woman than the size of her waist or the firmness of her breasts. Look in the mirror: What do you see? What you should see (and I very rarely tell people what they should think, feel, or do) is a woman who is sexual simply because she is a woman. See yourself through your partner's eyes. You are the one who smiles at him, who accepts him for who he is, who cuddles him when he is in despair, who enjoys being with him. All of these things make you sexually interesting to him. You have forgotten that most men want what women want: someone to love them. If that's what you are giving your partner in your relationship, that is what he responds to sexually. And how perfect is he? What about his spare tire or whatever else makes him who he is physically? Do you notice this whenever you see him, or do you see only the person he is?

If you have a partner who frequently criticizes your looks, this generally means there is something wrong with the relationship, not with how you look. I have seen couples in which the man harasses the woman about her weight, even to the point of saying that if she puts on even a couple of pounds, the relationship will end. In these instances, weight is not the issue. For anybody to put such extreme emphasis on physical appearance, there must be an underlying problem, and he, not you, needs to see a therapist.

Given that obesity is looming as a major health crisis in Western society, if you are overweight, yes, you may need to do something about it. But you should take control of your weight for yourself, not for your partner. Lose weight and get fit to be healthy and increase your chances of leading a long and active life, and then be happy with your body size and shape that this healthy lifestyle produces.

Practice Fantasizing

One factor that seems relevant to why low libido is more common among women than among men concerns the ability to have sexual fantasies. If sex drive is about anticipating sex, you have to think about sex in a pleasurable way to feel this interest. There are various estimates in sex therapy research as to how often men think about sex, with some claims that some men think about sex as often as every 15 minutes throughout the day. I'm not sure how accurate those estimates are, but men do seem to have sexual thoughts more often than women do. And if you don't ever think about sex, how can you happily anticipate it?

Women's difficulty with slipping into sexual fantasies probably relates to the fact that they tend not to masturbate as often as men do. More men than women masturbate, men who masturbate do so more frequently than women do, and women tend to be older when they discover masturbation, often after reading about it in a magazine somewhere. During masturbation, people use their mind to aid arousal, and this helps them develop the ability to have sexual fantasies and to stay focused on physical feelings during sexual activity. Without this practice, women can find it hard to tune in to sexual thoughts and feelings throughout their daily routines or during sex with a partner.

I have asked some women to try to boost their sex drive by deliberately trying to have a sexual fantasy during the day, and I've found mixed results. Some women found it relatively easy to do; for others, it was more of an effort and didn't always seem worth it; and still others couldn't be bothered, just as they couldn't be bothered with sex itself.

I would encourage you to practice developing sexual fantasies. Think about any books or movies that you have found even slightly arousing. Try to shut out all other thoughts and, in an almost lazy way, run through the scenes you recall. Don't try too hard, and if distracting thoughts occur, let them pass through your mind without focusing on them too long. Spend time thinking about the buildup of sexual tension in the story and follow the themes that are most interesting or appealing to you. You can practice in bed at night, like telling yourself a bedtime story, or do it while you are relaxing in the bathtub, sitting on a bus, or masturbating. Men, it seems, enjoy sexual fantasies at any time of the day or night and in all manner of situations, and the fantasies may last a few moments to several minutes, so it isn't really that odd for you to have sexual daydreams in places other than the privacy of your home.

Once you have been able to recapture some of the arousal you felt while reading sexual material or watching erotic movies, you can experiment with your own themes. Your fantasy may include your husband, or it may involve other men. Allow your mind to wander through a sexual story in which you are the central character. Sometimes getting a mild sexual buzz will be enough for you; at other times, fantasizing may produce a desire for self-stimulation or sex with your partner.

Some women feel guilty or disappointed that they find that thinking of other men produces sexual arousal but that thinking of their husband doesn't turn them on. This doesn't mean that you don't love your husband or that he isn't a good sex partner for you. True, it may be that seeing him step naked from the shower never sets your pulse racing in the same way that thinking about someone else might. If your husband is the man you love and trust, the man with whom, for all sorts of reasons, you want to spend the rest of your life, I know it would be great for you both if he evoked strong sexual feelings. For whatever reason, though, some women just do not find love and lust in the same man.

To me, the fact that thinking about other men turns you on means that you have the ability to fantasize. I don't believe that any fantasy about another man is bad if it helps to improve your sex life with the man you actually want to be with. Men fantasize about other women and rarely feel guilty about it, because they have been doing it ever since they began to masturbate.

It may help you to think about the difference between turning on *to* and turning on *with* your partner. Sometimes a woman with low sexual interest in her current partner explains her problem by saying that she believes that while she loves him, she isn't *in love* with him, because if she were in love she would be turned on by the sight or touch of him. This seems to me to be a very recent development in the way we think about relationships, and it represents the desire for a passionate relationship not just sexually but emotionally. But if you have a shared life that has much going for it, and you stand to lose more than you might gain if it were to end, loving and caring for each other can be a good basis for a happy life together. If you are not passionately aroused by your partner, turning on with him by using fantasies, positive thoughts, or foreplay techniques (including self-stimulation) can still lead to a satisfying sex life.

I also want to note here that you may feel worried if you find the thought of something like rape exciting. This does not mean that you wish to be raped or would enjoy being raped in reality. Sexual fantasies are no different from any other daydreams: They are chances to explore forbidden or unattainable territory with safety. It's surprising how many seemingly conservative people in happy, stable relationships have unusual, even bizarre, sexual fantasies that help fuel their sex life.

Stay Focused during Sex

Does your mind wander during sex? I know that the act is supposed to be so totally absorbing that pleasure washes over you and blots out all other thoughts, but this just isn't the case for many women I talk to. Women think about all sorts of mundane things at the most inappropriate moments. Suddenly, in a moment that her partner thinks is a time for wild passion, the thought will occur to her that she has to take little Johnny to the dentist tomorrow or that tonight is trash night, so the garbage needs to be taken out.

This doesn't happen just to women who are bored with whatever sexual activity is taking place, but boredom certainly doesn't help.

Although it's not conventional to think of sex as boring, it can be for some people—it's all a matter of individual differences and the mood of the moment. It isn't surprising that a bored woman may notice that the furniture needs dusting or start thinking about her grocery list. Sometimes, however, her mind can wander even when she's enjoying what is happening and is feeling quite aroused. And if she happens to say what is on her mind, her partner may become a little disconcerted.

I think a woman's wandering mind during sex has something to do with her ability to multitask, in other words, to keep track of several things at once. As I understand it, some differences in the structure of male and female brains means women find it easier to do several things at the same time, so from a woman's point of view, it isn't that odd that she would think of nonsexual things while engaged in sex.

Nevertheless, I also think this lack of focus is related to all the issues discussed so far. A woman needs time to get her mind into sex, so if the way sex is initiated isn't right for her, with a touch on the breasts or genitals instead of a more sensual introduction, she finds it difficult to get her mind focused and keep it focused. Then, if foreplay continues with stimulation that's irritating rather than soothing and arousing, and she doesn't get a lot out of intercourse, it isn't unreasonable for her mind to drift onto other things.

If you are having difficulty concentrating when you're having sex with your partner, the first thing I recommend is not to worry about it. You may need to discuss with your partner the issues of how you prefer sex to be initiated and what type of foreplay you prefer, but you can also develop strategies to shift your attention back to the main event. If you are able to enjoy fantasy, allow your mind to conjure images that focus your mind on sexual pleasure.

One of the simplest things to try is using your hands to stay aware of what is happening. Use touch to communicate how you feel about your partner: Stroke his face, run your hands down his back, gently play with other parts of his body. If you find it difficult to have sexual thoughts, try to think about how nice it is to be there with this man, how good his skin feels against yours, how warm and comforting his body is. This is the essence of relationship sex: tuning in to what is pleasant, soothing, and meaningful to you when you find it difficult to become aroused.

Don't Put Up with Painful Intercourse

I mentioned painful intercourse earlier, but I want to reinforce the importance of investigating this if it's a problem for you. For women with low libido, pain may be caused by lack of arousal and lack of lubrication, and in this case, the problem is easily remedied with an artificial lubricant. Make sure, however, to use a product that isn't likely to irritate your vagina; vaginal lubricants are available that are designed for this specific situation, and you can also use some products that can be used on a baby's genitals to soothe tender skin. If you're using condoms as contraception or are trying to get pregnant, use only approved vaginal lubricants. In any case, avoid hand creams or lotions, particularly anything that is perfumed.

There are, however, quite a few other physical problems that can cause penile thrusting to be painful. You need to find a medical practitioner with an interest in female sexual health who will take you seriously and not tell you it is all in your mind—whether the cause is stress or anxiety or a medical condition, the pain is in your vagina and must be investigated.

If you have low libido but can be aroused once you get into sex, you may not need a lubricant, but if you don't lubricate easily, anticipating pain or discomfort can depress your interest in sex even further. As with many other realities of sex, you don't see couples in movies needing to use lubricants, but it's a common part of the sexual routine for lots of women. Anything that makes sex more comfortable has got to be a good option to try.

YOUR SEXUAL RELATIONSHIP

Saying that a sexual relationship involves two people is stating the obvious. One of the few areas of agreement among sex therapists is that low libido is a problem for the couple, not just for one partner. What sex therapists can't seem to agree on, though, is whether relationship problems are the main cause of sexual difficulties, or vice versa. I don't think there is only one answer to this question, but even with couples such as Debbie and Alan, who had a sound emotional relationship and were doing the best they could for each other in their sexual relationship, Alan's sexual beliefs, expectations, and anxieties were influencing Debbie's interest in sex.

In this section, I want to explore your sexual relationship from your point of view. The following chapter provides your partner with the opportunity to think about what's happening from his perspective, and then we can move on to helping you work together to improve your sex life.

Take Responsibility for Affection

Once sex becomes unsatisfying, boring, or irritating, it's quite common for the woman's desire to avoid sex to spread into other areas of her intimate relationship with her partner. As the anti-libido cycle escalates, the woman finds herself avoiding hugging, cuddling, kissing, sitting on the sofa together to watch television, and so on because she thinks doing these things will encourage her partner to try for sex. This means the couple feels more and more distant from each other—and more and more lonely in the relationship.

Not surprisingly, this is the most common feeling men talk to me about. Yes, they would like to be having sex, but most say it's the fact that their partner almost cringes at their touch that distresses them the most.

If you find yourself in this situation, you can start to do something about it immediately. Tell your partner you are going to start giving him hugs, cuddles, and kisses sometimes, but he has to promise not to try to take it any further or not get upset if he does try for more and you make it clear you want only some affection. Try to give him a quick hug every day, then, as you relax with this, make it a longer cuddle. If you can do this more than once a day, you can take my word that eventually, he will get the idea that affection is not automatically a lead-in to sex.

I ask you to take responsibility for increasing affection for two reasons. First, you can choose the time and place, so you're not going to feel annoyed at being interrupted while you're busy. Second, because you have felt so guilty and powerless for so long, it will be great for your self-esteem to realize that you have such a positive role in your emotional life. It's also wonderful to realize that your partner loves you for you, not just for sex, and that it really isn't that difficult to help your partner feel loved and secure, just as you want to feel.

You can make the situation lighthearted—it doesn't have to be deadly serious. For example, if he's cuddling you and his hands start to wander, grab his hands, put his arms around you, and tell him, "Down, boy; remember this is just a cuddle," or whatever seems right to you. Don't act offended if he forgets himself sometimes; your reaction to him is an important part of the anti-libido cycle, too.

Getting some affection back into your relationship is at first more important than increasing your sexual frequency, because it changes the atmosphere between you to being more gentle, caring, and loving. This is important if you are going to build your sexual relationship using emotional/sensual sex.

Take Advantage of Any Feelings of Sexual Interest

Are there times when you feel like having sex but you don't let your partner know?

There are various reasons that a woman may not act on any feelings of sexual interest. She may worry that if she approaches her partner for some wildly raunchy sex, he will then expect her to do it regularly. Since she can't guarantee that she will feel the same way on a consistent basis, she ignores the impulse to seduce him.

Similarly, a woman who is recovering from a period of low sex drive, such as after the birth of a baby, may also not let her partner know of her occasional sexual interest because she's afraid he will think everything is back to normal. She knows this isn't the case, because women recovering from episodes of low drive typically have quite erratic patterns of sexual desire. While she may be keen one night, it could be weeks before that feeling returns.

In both of these cases, the simple answer is to go for it when the mood strikes you, but afterward, let your partner know, with some regret for you both, that you can't guarantee when you will feel that way again.

A woman also may not act on her sexual interest because she fears that her partner will interpret her behavior to mean that she feels very turned on and wants passionate sex, when in fact she may want sex for more emotional and sensual reasons. The best solution is to trust your feelings and be confident enough to say how you're feeling and what you need. "I'm not horny, but I want your body; I need to be close" is just one example of how to explain your intentions.

Another obstacle that may keep a woman from expressing her desire for sex is that in general, women are more tuned in to their partner's emotional states. This means that if he has said he's tired or for some reason she assumes he wouldn't be interested in sex, she won't make advances because she doesn't want to put him out. When this comes up in sex therapy, the reaction of a lot of men is "Please, please, let me be the one to decide whether or not I want sex!"

Not feeling confident to initiate sex, for any reason, can skew the perception of a woman's libido. In the case of one couple I saw who had different biological clocks, the husband felt that his wife had low libido because she wasn't keen when he was interested in the morning, and he had to make a lot of effort to get her to respond to his advances. When she explained that she did feel interested in the evening, but she knew he was tired and didn't want to bother him, the focus of their mismatched libido issue changed.

When a woman is prepared to try to initiate sex, she may find it difficult to be blatant about what she wants. She may give only indirect signals, which her partner often misses. One woman felt that by saying, "I'm going to bed now," she was inviting her husband to come with her for sex, but he said he didn't realize that that was any different from other nights when she went to bed early. Even in today's supercharged sexual atmosphere, you may feel uncomfortable about doing a striptease to get your husband's interest or taking the initiative by undressing him. Maybe the answer is to tell him, "When I say this or do that, it means I want to have sex with you."

Women seem to be more influenced by practical issues than men are. Although a woman may feel interested in sex, she can switch herself off when she realizes that the kids will be home soon, or it's late and tomorrow is an early start, or she has to prepare dinner because guests are due soon. It's a tricky situation, to be sure, but this could be the time to make sex about doing something cheeky and daring.

By not having sex on those occasions when you actually feel like it, you are limiting yourself to having sex when your partner initiates it. The chances that you'll always want sex at the same time he does aren't high, so you are losing those opportunities when sex is likely to be best for you. Although it's difficult for you to clearly signal when sex seems like a good idea, give it a try. A strategy that can overcome any embarrassment is to act out a role. Think of someone in the movies and imagine what she does in a seduction scene. By hamming it up as someone else, you can get past your own inhibitions, and eventually it will become easier to initiate sex as yourself.

Be Present with Your Partner during Sex

While there are men like Erin's husband, Steve, who aren't happy with anything less than an hour of passionate sex, a lot of the men who come with their wives for sex therapy say that more than anything, they want their partner to want to be with them during sex. Yes, it would be good for them if the women wanted to play erotic games, but missing out on these things isn't what's worrying them. They tell me that what distresses them the most when their partner lies there with a faraway look or tells them to hurry up is that they feel as if they're imposing themselves, and they know their partner doesn't want to be there with them. This is what leads to the feelings of loneliness and rejection the men talk about. They try hard to make sex better for their partner, not realizing that their best efforts are likely to make things worse.

Thus, while the woman is worried that she's letting her partner down, he is worried that he's doing the wrong thing by her, and sex becomes more complicated than it needs to be.

You can see why I believe the concept of relationship sex has a lot to offer couples who are caught up in the sexual illusion. Relationship sex means that the woman identifies and acts on her own reasons for wanting to have sex with her partner, and she can reassure him that she really does want to be there with him. If the couple knows that they care about each other, it isn't that difficult to give each other what they want. The woman can appreciate sensual sex with or without arousal, and the man can enjoy becoming aroused with her if he knows she's content to be present emotionally during sex. If you use some of the suggestions in the section on staying focused during sex, such as touching his face, running your hands across his body, or playing idly with his penis, he'll know you are there with him—and you are giving him what he wants.

Say No to Sex with Confidence

In all my years of clinical practice, I have talked with hundreds of women about motherhood, careers, sexuality, relationships—all areas of women's lives. The common thread running through all these discussions is *guilt*. Women feel guilty if they go to work and leave their children, if they take a day off from work to look after sick children, if they can't devote enough time to their own parents, if they don't enjoy motherhood 100 percent . . . and the list goes on.

Men don't seem to embrace guilt with such enthusiasm. I've found that men are much more likely to assess situations in terms of their own adequacy, so the more common bad feeling among men is *inadequacy*, which brings its own problems.

Most of the women I talk with tell me they feel awful when they say no to sex. Although they may also be irritated, annoyed, or sad, guilt is the main reaction. This seems to happen across all types of relationships. Erin's husband, Steve, was a very difficult and demanding person who expected sex several times a week and wouldn't settle for anything less than an hour of intense sexual activity, but for years Erin felt guilty that she was letting him down by not giving him the sex life he wanted. Richard, who was depressed and needed sex daily in order to feel reassured that Anne loved him, claimed that she didn't really care about him when she said no, thus making her feel guilty.

Even when the man is extremely gentle, caring, and considerate and genuinely understands and accepts his wife's lower interest (like Debbie's husband, Alan), the woman still feels guilty that she is depriving him of the sex life she feels he deserves. That may be even more true in these situations because he is so supportive and understanding. It's common for a woman to explain to me that her husband has been so patient, that he isn't the problem. She can't understand how he has stayed with her; she feels terrible that he is missing out all the time.

What does feeling guilty imply? It implies that you believe you are doing something wrong and that your needs and feelings are not as important as your partner's. Realistically, what are you doing that is so bad? You haven't chosen to have low libido; in fact, I know how much you would like to feel more sexual desire than you do. Life would be simpler for you if you had as strong a desire for sex as your partner does. You are not to blame for what's happening in your sexual relationship.

Feeling guilty also implies a belief that if your partner doesn't have sex when he wants it, he will suffer in some way, and it's your responsibility not to let that happen. Let's look at this more objectively. Yes, it's true that if he feels aroused and doesn't have an orgasm, he may feel sexually frustrated. I'm sure, however, that he has felt sexually frustrated many times and has always survived. If you really do not feel like having sex, and he feels overcome with frustration, the simplest solution is in his own hands. If, like Margaret's husband, Ed, he feels he shouldn't have to masturbate, that is his choice. I agree that it's not the most desirable solution for him, but it does resolve his immediate physical need—and his sexual frustration is his responsibility, not yours.

A good sexual relationship is based on mutual respect, mutual compromise, and give-and-take based on mutual caring and consideration. It cannot be based on obligation. If you feel guilty when you say no, your sexual relationship is out of balance; you are focusing on what he wants, or what you think he wants, rather than on your own feelings. You can't develop your sex drive based on guilt.

Challenge Your Partner's Inappropriate Reaction to Your Refusal

We have seen that there are various elements in the anti-libido cycle that combine to develop differences in libido into a significant problem for some couples. Often, before a couple even begins to think they have a sexual problem, these elements begin to influence the sexual relationship and set the problem-making process in motion. How a man reacts when his partner says no to sex can play a vital role in escalating the situation from an ordinary issue of differences in some areas of sex into a major point of conflict.

There are certainly many couples like Debbie and Alan who are concerned about their different levels of sexual interest, but the man reacts to the woman's disinterest with understanding and support. These men tend to come to sex therapy with their wife from the beginning and have tried to avoid putting any pressure on them for sex. Unfortunately, some men react in quite inappropriate ways, although this is not always a true indicator of how they are feeling.

Does your partner simply roll over and go to sleep if you say no to sex, not even wanting to cuddle if it isn't going to lead to sex? Does he persist in touching you so that in the end, it's easier to give in to get some peace?

Does he become sullen, so you know that things will be very strained for the next few days or so until you have sex? Does he tell you, even plead with you, that it has been days since you've had sex, and he's really frustrated and can't sleep properly, so don't be mean? Does he become critical, verbally abusive, or even very angry? Does he tell you there must be something wrong with you, and you should see someone to get fixed up?

If he reacts in any of these ways, how do you feel at the time? Resigned? Hurt? Inadequate? Resentful? Angry? Frustrated? What messages does his reaction give you about yourself? Do you believe that there is something wrong with you but that he is normal and doesn't have a problem? Do you feel that he wants you only for sex and doesn't care about you as a person?

The sad thing is that many of the men I talk with do not view their wife just as a sex object. Behind these inappropriate reactions are often feelings of hurt, rejection, and inadequacy, which he has trouble talking about with you. When the sexual relationship runs into trouble, men have no idea how to go about solving the problem, apart from trying more of the ideas they get about sex from movies or men's magazines.

There are, then, two more features of the anti-libido cycle operating here—poor communication and misinterpretation—and it's in these areas that you can bring about some significant changes quickly.

First, you need to know that you have the right to feel the way you do about sex and that your partner has to understand and respect your point of view as much as he expects you to consider his. No one is right or wrong when libidos are mismatched. Second, if your relationship is basically sound, you need to recognize that there is a good chance that behind your partner's reactions, there are feelings that he has a lot of trouble talking with you about.

Therefore, it's not a matter of your accepting all the responsibility for the problems in your sexual relationship. The problem is shared between you, and you can begin to deal with it by clearly and confidently talking with your partner about how you see things. It's important that you state the situation from your point of view. Using I-language ("I feel," "I think") rather than the more critical and judgmental you-language ("you are," "you do") can be useful, but it's more important that you genuinely try to explain your views and are open to understanding his. Instead of making a direct accusation by saying something like, "You don't care about me; you are only interested in sex," you could say, "When you roll over and ignore me when I'm not interested in sex, I feel as if you don't care about me at all." Instead of "The way you talk to me, how can you ever expect me to want sex with you?" you can try, "When you talk to me the way you do, I feel upset and hurt and even less like having sex."

Once you have been able to tell your partner how you feel, you can then ask him what he thinks or feels. He may find it easier to answer if you ask him what he thinks, since he may find it difficult to say what he feels. You could try, "What do you think about all this? Do you worry that I don't love you? What do you think the problem is? How do you really feel when I am not interested in sex?" and so on.

If this sounds stilted, you may want to put these ideas into your own words. It may be difficult for you to challenge your partner, but the majority of men I talk to are more bothered by feeling rejected by their wife than they are by the physical lack of sex, so he may be quite relieved to be given the chance to talk things over calmly with you.

If, despite your best efforts, he continues to react in a demeaning way whenever you don't respond to his advances, there may be little chance that your relationship can provide you with the warmth and security you are seeking.

DO YOU STILL FEEL THAT HAVING SEX MEANS GIVING IN?

Does what you've read so far make sense to you? Can you see ways of using what I've discussed so that sex seems a better option than it did before? Or do you feel, "That's all very well, but why should I do all this for him?"

If you feel that there's nothing for you to gain by working with your partner on your sexual relationship, it may well be that there has been too much damage to your emotional relationship to hold any hope for the future. In order to solve sexual problems, there has to be enough caring and goodwill between you to make you want to improve your sex life and enhance your good feelings for each other.

If those feelings aren't there, it will be very difficult to make changes in your sex life. At this point, it may be helpful for you both to see a qualified counselor who can help you explore the implications of this for your relationship.

MOVING FORWARD

Go back over your notes and see if you can identify the issues that are most relevant to your particular situation. What have you found out about yourself? What points need to be discussed with your partner? What questions would you like to ask him? Then, read through the next chapter and see if you can predict his responses to the issues raised there.

CHAPTER 10

IT TAKES TWO

THIS CHAPTER IS FOR THE PARTNER OF THE WOMAN WITH LOW LIBIDO. I have found that most men are more than willing to be involved in the process of change and want the opportunity to think through the issues that are bothering them.

The good news is that it's highly likely that you are not doing anything significantly wrong and that improving your sexual relationship may be easier than you may have feared. You might find it useful to have a pen and paper handy and jot down points and ideas as they occur to you.

BE PREPARED TO BE PART OF THE SOLUTION

A man's role in his partner's lack of interest in sex can vary tremendously. Sometimes he has rigid ideas of what he expects in a sexual relationship and puts pressure on his wife to fulfill his unrealistic expectations. More commonly, he has tried to understand his wife's feelings and has wracked his brain to find solutions to help her, with no success. Often, no matter what the situation, it can be difficult for the man to get past his belief that he is the normal one and that his wife has the problem, so she is the only one who can fix things.

The truth is that it's very difficult for your partner to solve this problem on her own. Whether she has to challenge the rigid stereotypes of normal female sexuality or struggle with serious issues arising from past psychological trauma, she needs your love, interest, and support as well as your willingness to adapt your sexual expectations to help her reach her sexual potential.

Avoid Blame

It can be very confusing for a man to be in relationship with a woman who seems to continually reject his sexual advances. Typically, men who come to counseling with their wife are caught between the frustration of not having their own needs met and the fear that they are letting their partner down in some way. A man may also worry that she doesn't find him sexually attractive anymore. Does she have a sexual problem, and that is why she doesn't want sex, or is it him—is he doing something wrong? Maybe he comes too soon or his penis isn't big enough or he just isn't a good lover?

Unfortunately, a lot of men can find it difficult to deal with emotional issues such as these. Rather than talking to his partner about how he feels and sharing his own feelings of self-doubt and rejection, a man in this position is more likely to avoid all of this by declaring there is nothing wrong with him and that it's all her problem. "I'm fine," he says, "my sex drive is normal, I want sex every week/day, so you see a sex therapist and get yourself fixed."

If this is the position you've been taking, I would like you to give it some further thought. While it may certainly be true that your sex drive is normal, this doesn't mean that your partner is abnormal because hers is different.

If you have read the earlier parts of this book, you can see that sex drive isn't just about feeling hot or sexually frustrated. It's also important that what happens during sexual activity be enjoyable and acceptable. It's quite possible that although the sexual activities you enjoy are quite normal, what you want and expect during sex isn't what your partner wants and expects.

At this point, then, the sensible question is not, Who's to blame? Rather, the issue is whether your relationship with your partner is important enough to you that you are prepared to accept that her needs are different from yours and that you may need to change some of your sexual ideas and behaviors so that sex can be a more agreeable, enjoyable activity for her.

This doesn't mean that you are or have been a poor lover. It's almost impossible not to be influenced by books, movies, and magazines, all of which promote the same stereotyped image in which arousal, orgasm, and lots of activity are essential ingredients for great sex. Women are just as influenced by these images as men are, so they usually don't have the confidence to explain how they feel about sex and what they need in order to become interested in and enjoy sex.

Blaming yourself or your partner for the current tension in your sexual relationship is a complete waste of time. If you want your relationship to continue, you and your partner need to work together to solve the problem.

If, however, you aren't prepared to be involved, nothing can change in your sexual relationship, and you need to discuss this with your partner so you can both consider the implications for your future.

Evaluate Your Own Sex Drive

Just as women differ in terms of their levels of interest in sex, men vary in how often they would like sex. Some men are happy with sex every now and then, some would like it once or twice a week, some want it every day, and others tell me they would like it more than once a day. How often would you like to have sex? Is this the level of activity you hope for, but you can be content if you don't get it, or do you feel you need to have sex this often and wouldn't be happy if it's less frequent?

The problem is that if your partner believes that you must have sex at a certain frequency, she starts to feel pressured to have sex that often, regardless of how she feels. As I explained when I described the stages of the anti-libido cycle earlier in this book, once she feels she is expected to have sex, it then becomes something she does to please you rather than for her own enjoyment. Sex can actually become a chore, so her interest decreases.

Most men I talk to in your position are in a real dilemma. You want sex because it's enjoyable and satisfying both physically and emotionally, and there's nothing odd about wanting to do something that is pleasurable as often as possible. Yet, your partner doesn't get the same pleasure from sex and clearly doesn't want it as often as you do. The problem is, the average man I talk to doesn't want his partner to have sex just to please him; he wants her to want it as much and get as much pleasure from it as he does.

The fact is, though, that she doesn't, and she may never feel the same way about sex as you do, so you're in a difficult position. If you let your partner know what you want, will she perceive that as an expectation and feel pressured? If you don't let her know, will she assume you don't want sex and just let it pass, so that you have sex only every now and then?

Resolving some of this confusion lies with you. When you say how often you want sex, is that what you want or what you expect? For example, a lot of men tell their wives that they would like sex every day, yet they don't let on that they don't really expect it that often. The men explain to me that if they tell their partner they would be quite happy with sex once a week, she will still say no some of the time, so they could end up having sex much less often than that. Like these men, do you try to keep up the pressure and approach your partner at every opportunity in the hope that you may get sex somewhere near as frequently as you'd like? While I can see the logic of that line of thinking, I doubt that it's helping the situation. Be honest with your partner and work with her on trying to find ways of having sex as frequently as is reasonable for both of you. If you keep the goal too high, she may just give up.

If you do want sex every day or more often, and you're not prepared to settle for less, what messages are you giving your partner about her importance as a person, not just someone who should be giving you sex?

Rethink Your Ideas about Sex Drive

Generally, I find that men and women have similar beliefs about what sex drive should be. Like the woman herself, the man usually expects her to experience a physical need for sex and desire for him as a sexual partner. He expects to see evidence of this in her keenness to initiate and participate in sex with him.

It can be hard for you to understand that your partner rarely, if ever, has the same sexual urges that you do; she may feel that it wouldn't bother her if she never had sex again. Yet she may get aroused and come to orgasm when she does agree to have sex, which would certainly add to your confusion as to why she never seems to want it. On the other hand, if she usually finds sexual touch irritating, how can that be possible, when everyone knows that it should be intensely pleasurable?

The challenge in these circumstances is for you and your partner to figure out what will help her decide that sex is a good idea. I know of some men whose partner doesn't approach them for sex but who find she usually has an orgasm when he makes the first move, who will try the strategy of not initiating sex for several weeks in the hope that sexual frustration will drive their partner to initiate it, but this rarely works. Sexual drive and sexual response just don't seem to be linked in women in the same way they are in men.

This means that it's likely that you will continue to be the one who makes most of the advances. Some men feel hurt by this because they feel that the lack of approach from their partner is a sign that the woman doesn't love them or find them attractive. This is one of the misinterpretations that lead to so much trouble when there are differences in libido. There are two basic reasons why your partner may not try to seduce you: (1) She rarely or never thinks of it, or (2) if she does think about it, she worries that if she initiates sex, you will think she is hotter and keener than she really is when she may only want quiet, brief sex.

Unfortunately, because the responsibility for initiating sex rests with you, you are the one who risks being turned down, and it's hard to not feel hurt about being rejected, particularly when it happens often. Be honest with your partner about how you feel and let her know you will settle for cuddling if sex isn't an option. But that doesn't answer the burning question of how to make sex a more attractive possibility for her. What can you do that will increase the chances that she will say yes rather than no?

Expand Your Ideas about Good Sex

By now, you have probably realized that what we've come to think of as good sex in our society may in fact be part of the problem for people with low libido.

We have seen that mood, in particular, affects women's interest in sex and their ability to become aroused and have an orgasm. Since it's unrealistic to expect that your partner will always be in a happy, buoyant mood and never feel tired, stressed, or down, it makes sense to develop a more flexible attitude about what you seek in sexual activity. If you believe your partner should get aroused, be very active, want to experiment, and have an orgasm whenever you have sex, you may actually be making the act less enjoyable for her. This emphasis on arousal and orgasm can, from a woman's point of view, be irritating, seem too much like hard work, or distract her from other aspects of sex, such as emotional intimacy, which for her may be more satisfying than physical release.

Relationship sex—that is, sex in which behavioral goals such as orgasm or oral sex are not the main aim, and the focus is on emotional contact through the physical senses—is lovemaking in a real sense. Because the focus isn't on specific actions or outcomes, such as orgasm, this lovemaking can be very brief or last for lengthy periods; it may involve only simple caresses or be expressed in many different forms of kissing, touch, and sexual position. It may result in orgasm, or it may not. Your partner may be very still; she may even fall asleep as the gentleness soothes her and the warmth and security of intercourse reassures her. This type of sensual and emotional sex is very satisfying to many women.

The problem is that your partner probably lacks the confidence to tell you that this is the type of sex she needs when she's very tired or pre-occupied with other life stresses, and you may believe there is something wrong with her when she wants to be very still during sex. Can you adjust your ideas about good sex to take into account this range of what might make sex good for your partner?

Be Flexible in the Way You Initiate Sex

An important way in which you can make sex more attractive to your partner is to rethink how you approach her. One of the great myths of modern times is that the way to get a woman interested in sex is to fondle her breasts or stimulate her between the legs. Even when a man begins with a cuddle, it isn't long before his hands wander to those areas. This may be fine for a woman who is already sexually interested, perhaps because you've been watching a movie together with sex scenes that appeal to her, or her thoughts have turned to sex for other reasons.

In general, though, playing with her breasts and genitals is likely to be more irritating than arousing if that is the first indication she has that this is what you're seeking. This is particularly true if you and she have spent little time together in the preceding day or so, with no quality time to chat and catch up as a couple.

Foreplay for the woman is first a feeling of closeness and intimacy, so that what happens long before sex is considered has a lot to do with whether or not she is interested. If you sat around while your partner made dinner, cleaned up the kitchen, and coped with the kids; you both sat silently watching television for hours before going to bed; or there's been a disagreement or you've been critical of her, and this hasn't been resolved before you approach her for sex, your chances of her being interested in sex are pretty slim.

The other thing to keep in mind is that a woman's interest in sex and her ability to become aroused and have an orgasm are influenced by her mood and perhaps by where she is in her menstrual cycle. This helps to explain some of the frustrating contradictions in her behavior. Sometimes, she will respond to a more direct, passionate approach—she has had a good day, maybe she is at a good time in her cycle, and you and she have been getting along well. On other occasions, even a slow, sensual approach seems to provoke annoyance. And then there are the truly confusing occasions when she initially says no and gets edgy when you touch her, but as you hold her and caress her, she slowly becomes interested and eventually is rather keen.

What should you do when your partner initially seems uninterested in your overtures if past experience has taught you that this can sometimes change? By starting with gentle cuddling, massage, talking over the events of the day before you directly approach her for sex, you can give her time to settle down from the stresses of the day and turn her attention to you, as well as get more in tune with her body so that she can be clearer about what she actually wants. If she isn't interested when you first move to more direct sexual touch, you can return to sensual foreplay, and she may be more responsive after more time to unwind. However, once it's clear that further attempts to get her interested are getting her more annoyed rather than changing her mind, it's time to stop.

Another situation that often causes confusion arises when you do all the things you think are right—take the time to relax with her, maybe even take her to dinner and have an intimate chat over a leisurely bottle of wine—and she still isn't interested! The problem here is that throughout the meal, the massage, or whatever options you have decided to try, your partner is thinking, "I know what he wants; when this is over, he wants/expects me to have sex." Once again, it doesn't work for her because that feeling of expectation makes her feel pressured.

Your partner needs to feel that special nights out, cuddles, caresses, quiet chats, massages, and even weekends away are not merely ploys to get her to have sex but are ways to spend quality time with her. She wants to be able to enjoy these activities without the "threat" of sex, and she needs to feel she has a choice in the matter. Sometimes these things will lead to sex, and sometimes they won't. She needs to feel that she can say, "This is nice, but it's all I feel like at the moment," without you reacting badly. If all intimate moments or special times together lead to attempts at sex by you, ultimately she will avoid these as well, and this heightens the feelings of rejection and isolation that do so much damage.

It would be nice if sex were as simple as we see it portrayed in the movies: You are interested, make some sexual suggestions, and touch her erotically, and she is soon responding with enthusiasm. In real life, it isn't like that, and the time, the place, and the manner in which you approach your partner for sex are all-important aspects of whether or not it happens.

Rethink the Connection between Affection and Sex

It's particularly important to separate the expression of affection from attempts to initiate sex. Some men tell me that it's all very well to say that women need affection without it always leading to sex, but that's not what they are like. As one man said, he wasn't brought up with a lot of affection; his father was a hardworking man who believed that real men didn't hug each other and didn't need all that sissy stuff. Besides, once you start cuddling, it's natural to want to touch her breasts or genitals and maybe try for sex. Why can't she just relax and go along with it?

There is one simple response to this point of view. You are asking your wife to respect your sexual needs and be prepared to make an effort to give you what you want. If you expect your relationship to work, there needs to be mutual respect and a desire to meet your partner's needs. This means that you need to treat her affectionate needs with the same respect with which you want her to treat your sexual needs. Despite the fact that we live in a highly sexualized society that places a great deal of importance on sex, this doesn't mean that sexual needs are more important than other needs in a relationship.

It makes sense for you to listen when your partner tells you what helps her feel more interested in sex; if you don't, it shouldn't be surprising if she finds it difficult to respond to your sexual needs. Most women with low libido say that having more affection without sex helps them feel more loved and secure, and this helps their interest in sex at other times. I'm sure you are open to solving the tension in your sexual relationship, and it will make a significant difference to your partner if you work on this issue with her.

Separate Sexual Wants from Sexual Needs

Some men feel relieved by the concept of relationship sex. Discovering that sex in a long-term relationship need not be about what you actually do or how long the sexual session lasts, but rather about the emotional and sensual aspects of your relationship with your partner, can lift a huge burden from a man who worries that he is letting his partner down with his sexual performance.

Is this how you feel, or do you feel that the idea of relationship sex is totally unreasonable and that quiet, sensual sex will never be enjoyable for you?

Given the emphasis in our society on sexual techniques and passionate and erotic relationships, it certainly wouldn't be surprising if this idea takes a bit of getting used to. But there is a difference between what you may want during sex and what you feel you just can't do without, and while some men eventually make the shift, others say that unless they get what they are looking for, the relationship is in trouble. Perhaps you feel like Erin's husband, Steve, who wouldn't accept sex that didn't include encounters lasting an hour or more, with a variety of techniques and positions, or Margaret's husband, Ed, who believed that he got very little out of sex unless she got very aroused and had strong orgasms. Some men can't imagine sex without common techniques such as oral sex, and they find it difficult to accept that when a woman is tired or stressed, sex can be better for her without the pressure to get aroused and come to orgasm.

In sex therapy, it's common for a man to say that he needs to feel that his wife strongly desires him in the way he has seen women lust after men in erotic movies. Some couples for whom this is the main issue do very well sexually in most other ways—she can come to orgasm easily, for example, and she enjoys a wide range of sexual techniques and positions—but because she doesn't come on to him in a hot and exciting way, he remains unhappy. Do you believe you can't enjoy your sexual relationship unless this happens?

There are men whose sexual needs are more unusual, such as Martin, who needed his partner to let him stare at her genitals for several minutes so that he could get aroused. Do you have a particular need that you want your partner to meet, and do you feel annoyed or hurt if she feels she can't participate in your type of sex? You may feel your partner is being unreasonable, particularly if your need seems quite commonplace, such as having her dress in teddies or other sexy lingerie. But I have seen some men who say that if their partner really loved them, they would want to be involved in less common activities, such as cross-dressing, bondage, dressing up in leather, or using only silk sheets on the bed. The problem is that although this sexual diversity is now considered normal, there is nothing wrong with your partner if she finds these things unappealing or even distasteful.

You and your partner face some difficult issues if you feel you can't accept sex without a particular erotic activity, or you require her to desire you in an erotic way, but she doesn't find those activities enjoyable and her sex drive is more sensual and restrained. In the end, the strength of your commitment to each other will hopefully help you talk the issue through and develop solutions that are acceptable to both of you. The alternative to this is that one of you "wins" and the other "loses," which can breed resentment and may be toxic to the emotional health of your relationship.

Be Considerate When She Says No

We've seen that a number of factors contribute to differences in sex drive becoming a major problem for a couple. One of the most important factors is the way you deal with your partner's reluctance to have sex, and what this means for her.

There are basically three categories of response you can choose from when your partner isn't interested in sex. The first is to recognize her right to her own feelings and to simply accept her answer and be content with some affection instead. If this happens from the earliest stages of your relationship, there is every chance that the differences in desire won't become a problem, because a healthy level of give-and-take usually develops over the years. Women can choose to have sex to please their partner and have that be okay for them, but whether this happens depends on how good she feels in the relationship generally. If your partner feels appreciated by you because you understand and support her needs, it can be easy and satisfying for her to sometimes have sex with you just because she wants to make you happy. In my experience, this situation of mutual sensitivity to each other's needs is common with couples whose libidos are out of kilter, and as a result, the couple develops an adequate sex life.

The second category of response is much more problematic. If you often become annoyed, sulky, withdrawn, or angry when your partner says no to sex, you are giving her the message that how she feels doesn't matter, that your sexual needs are more important, and that she is being unfair and unreasonable in not giving you sex. If you react this way every time she says no, think about what you are asking her to do. You may not consciously expect your partner to let you use her body, but this is the message she receives. She may also get the idea that there is something wrong with her (she is frigid, cold, and inhibited) because she doesn't always want to have sex when you feel like it. But how can she be warm and loving when you seem to be treating her as an object, not a person?

From your partner's point of view, if your sexual relationship is to have a chance of improving, she has to feel that she is more important to you than sex. *In order to be able to sincerely and happily say yes when sex is okay for her, she has to be able to comfortably say no when it's not.* With your reaction, you are making her feel she has no choice, so instead of sexual feelings, she has resentment and hurt.

If you've been reacting to her this way for some time, her interest in sex at this stage is probably nonexistent. It's important that you think about how you are going to deal with this over the coming months as you both try to address the problems arising from your mismatched sex drives. I agree that it may be disappointing that you may not have sex very often during that time, but irritation and anger are not healthy ways of coping. Try saying something like, "That's okay, Sweetheart, I understand. Let's take our time, and we'll work it out."

The third way that some men react is by withdrawing from sex. These are men who don't want to pressure their partner in any way and can't consider having sex unless their wife is active and willing. If you react in this way, your concern for your partner's feelings is understandable and commendable. The dilemma is that if you both avoid sex, the problem isn't being addressed. While your partner feels guilty that you are missing out on sex, she doesn't know what to do about it. If you can accept that she may never initiate sex and are prepared to take the risk of rejection and continue to let her know when you would like sex, you will both have the opportunity to explore new ways of conducting your sexual relationship. You may find that your version of relationship sex is a very satisfying alternative to no sex at all.

Regardless of how you usually respond, if your partner always says no to sex, so that it rarely or never happens, it's understandable if you have trouble remaining calm and philosophical about it. When needs and wants are very different, an easy solution isn't always available. Nevertheless, if you want to give your relationship a chance, being accepting when she says no is an important way that you may help to turn your sex life around.

Recognize Your Emotional Needs

The sad thing about quite a few of the men that I talk to is that no matter how they react outwardly to their partner's refusal of sex, they often feel hurt, rejected, inadequate, and lonely. Unfortunately, they often don't recognize these feelings or know what to do with them. Because men may use sex as their way of expressing love, they feel their partner is rejecting their love when they're turned down. For many men, this is more important than not having their sexual needs met.

The problem can extend beyond sex into all areas of affection. For many men, casual touching in a sexual way, such as playfully fondling their partner's breasts or touching them between the legs, is their way of letting their partner know how much they care. When a woman reacts with irritation, a man may interpret that as meaning she doesn't love him.

This issue can be resolved with a little bit of understanding on both sides. If you are feeling hurt and rejected, tell her. Don't whine about it, as in, "You don't love me; you never let me touch you; you're being unfair," which puts the problem on her. You could try talking to her in the following way: "We haven't been having sex much lately, and I'm worried about what the problem is. When you turn me down when I want sex, I feel you don't care about me or that you don't find me attractive any more. Sometimes, I get worried you may even want to leave me. Can you tell me what the problem is?"

I recognize that this sounds stiff and formal, so you'll want to use your own words. However, it's important that you describe the situation from your point of view and that you speak gently, not in an angry and confrontational manner. Your partner can then try to tell you what she's feeling—and you both must be prepared to listen to each other and want to understand each other's point of view.

What can come out of this type of dialogue is not a mudslinging match of accusation and counteraccusation but the recognition that you are both feeling hurt by what's happening in your sexual relationship. Don't waste any more time in anger and conflict, which is always useless and counterproductive if you really want your relationship to work out.

Learning to express your love in nonsexual ways is an important step in solving the sexual problem. Let your partner know that her saying no to sex isn't the real problem and that just cuddling or spending time with her (no sexual strings attached) would mean more to you than her giving in to sex just to keep the peace. Respecting her right not to have to behave sexually just to reassure you will help free sex from much of the tension that's currently depressing it and will make it more likely that you will get the loving reassurance you're seeking.

Let Go of Your Resentment

Some men are quite open about their resentment of the fact that by rejecting a man's sexual advances, a woman has the power to deny him sexual pleasure. These men say that it's all very well to tell women that they don't have to do things they don't want to do, but isn't that being unfair to men? Doesn't that mean that the woman is then in control of the sexual relationship—that it all goes her way and not his?

One young man became quite agitated about this in our session. "It's not fair," he said. "Sometimes I really want sex, and she just isn't interested. It really annoys me that she can dish out sex to suit her, and I just have to put up with it. It's like she's the boss. Doesn't what I want count?"

Some men resent the connection that many women make between how well the couple is getting along and her desire for sex. "It's like she rewards me for being good and punishes me for being bad," said one man. "If I do the right things, help with the kids and all that, then she'll probably have sex with me, but if I don't, it's no go. That really annoys me." In chapter 7, Sean described the way his wife's sex drive took a dive if he didn't help with domestic chores as making him "jump through hoops" to get sex.

This view that sex may be a tradeoff in a relationship is sometimes reinforced by what the woman herself says: "Why should I give you sex after the way you've treated me all day? Forget it!" Rather than consciously using sex as a means of getting what she wants, she believes she is merely stating the obvious. It isn't as if she feels like sex but is deliberately holding back because she wants to punish her partner—her annoyance, resentment, or anger makes the idea of sex completely unacceptable.

I certainly agree that compromise is an essential part of a good sexual relationship, but healthy compromise has to be based on goodwill and spring from the happy, caring nature of the relationship. If you believe your partner is using sex as power or punishment, the question to ask is, Why? Is your relationship so bereft of mutual caring and genuine concern for each other's happiness and welfare that sex *does* operate as something to be traded rather than something to be shared?

More commonly, I find that this is a good example of the differences between male and female sexuality. Men often see sex as independent of other parts of the relationship. A woman will express indignant surprise that he could even consider sex if they have had an argument that hasn't been resolved, and his response is likely to be, "What's that got to do with it?" or "But it's a good way to make up!"

When this situation arises, usually neither party means to be inconsiderate or insensitive, and the man genuinely believes that the woman would get a lot out of sex even if things are tense between them. However, I have met some men who are hurt or angry that their partner isn't prepared to have sex irrespective of whether they enjoy it or not. One man told me that he does things for her that he doesn't enjoy or would prefer not to do, so why can't she do this for him? He has to get up at 5:30 a.m. to go to work to earn money to support the family, and he hates doing that, so why is it any different for her having sex? Another man said that although he realized it wasn't politically correct in this day of women's rights, what was the big deal about her having sex when he wanted it, when it was only going to take a few minutes of her time?

It's always a challenge when this issue arises in sex therapy. It's the situation in which I am most likely to be accused of being anti-male when I explain how difficult it is to engage in sexual activity of any kind when you are feeling emotionally distant or upset with your partner. I explain that I also take this view when a man has the lower libido (although, of course, it's easier for the woman to allow her body to be used when she isn't interested than it is for the man). I can only state my belief that there is a world of difference between doing the dishes, or whatever, as part of the expectations in a relationship and engaging in unwanted sexual activity.

Your sexual needs are not your partner's responsibility, and sex is not a right in a relationship—those days are long gone. Your dilemma is to work on how to encourage your partner to *want* to be more involved, and if that feels like giving in to her and letting her have her way, then in my view, that suggests that there are other relationship issues to be addressed before I would expect to see much change in the sexual arena.

In the end, it depends on what type of relationship you both want. If your partner is prepared to have sex as a means of maintaining the marriage, and she sees this as merely another chore to perform, that is certainly her right. It is also your right to hold the view that your partner should be prepared to satisfy you sexually and that she is being unreasonable if she won't. However, for many women, this simply isn't enough. Without the emotional quality they are seeking in a relationship, a woman may decide she is better off on her own.

If you do love your partner and want your relationship to continue, you will get much further with this problem if you think about why you love her and how to build on what you already have, because strengthening your emotional relationship remains your best bet to build your sexual relationship. And isn't it a great thing that she wants to have an emotional relationship with you? It wouldn't be so good if she were saying that she didn't care about you at all!

Encourage Her Attempts to Change

Sometimes a man feels his partner isn't trying hard enough to improve their sexual relationship. This issue often arises after the couple has been working on the problem for a while. Although he believes that he is trying, he really can't see much changing sexually with his partner. He thinks, I'm making an effort; why isn't she? This can mean that either he thinks she isn't making an effort to change fast enough or he believes that she isn't making an effort to do the things he thinks are important.

It surprises me how often a woman tells me during her first session that her partner expects her to have all the answers when she gets home. It seems that he believes there is some mental switch in her head that only needs to be flicked on. When the couple comes to the sessions together, I usually explain that if the woman has no libido and is getting very little out of sex when she does have it, it will take months of working together before there is likely to be any significant change. Usually, the change is gradual and is more about the woman recognizing her own methods of finding sex an appealing option than about a sudden flowering of hot sexual desire.

The initial effort the woman makes in developing her interest in sex is to increase activities such as sitting next to her husband during the evening, having sex more often, exploring what's in it for her at the emotional or sensual level, and so on. While some men are delighted with these changes, others think they are unimportant, and she should be working on becoming very enthusiastic about sex or doing more erotic activities.

One of the most difficult cases I have seen was Steve and Erin, whom we have met several times so far. They had been married for more than 20 years when they came to see me, and Steve's complaint was that in all those years, Erin had made very little effort to have a normal sex life. As we have seen before, Steve's idea of normal was that sex should happen at least three times a week, the sessions should last for an hour or more, and Erin should demonstrate that she was hotly keen for it and be very active and responsive throughout. In Steve's view, because this wasn't happening, Erin clearly had a serious sexual dysfunction. In fact, Erin did enjoy sex, and in the past she had been happy to have sex a couple of times a week, but now the pressure she felt from Steve turned her off.

Nevertheless, Erin said she was prepared to try to please her husband, and she would begin each therapy session with what she felt were her achievements. None of these changes was ever good enough for Steve, and when she reported they had had sex several times since the previous session, he would say things like, "You don't call that making an effort, surely," or when Erin was pleased about enjoying sex, he would say, "You can't think that was good sex; what's wrong with you?" When I tried to explain to Steve that if he didn't give her some credit for the changes she was making, she would eventually give up, he thought I was being too soft. In the end, Erin decided to just go along with having sex a couple of times a week and put up with his complaints, so ultimately, neither was happy.

What are you asking your partner to do to demonstrate she is "making an effort"? Do you believe she should start giving you the sex you want because you have started to make some of the changes she has asked for? Sometimes, a man will come in to the second session and say that for the past week, he has helped with the children, cooked dinner, or whatever, but she isn't any more interested in sex, so it's a waste of time.

Do you mean that even if she is agreeing to sex more often, she isn't putting enough effort into wanting it? This is like asking you to get an erection even though the right things aren't happening to turn you on—and you know how difficult that can be. Or do you mean that although she is having sex more often and enjoying it more, there is nothing in it for you because it's too boring?

Similarly, some men complain that their partner is still making excuses to avoid having sex, with the implication that this is something unreasonable or mean. Rather than making this accusation, the obvious thing to do is to ask why she may want or need to make an excuse to avoid sex. If she's making excuses, there is likely to be a sensible reason. Are you prepared to work with her and try to understand what the reason is?

I can understand that it must be frustrating for you if you haven't been having much sex for some time, and you are worried that time is passing. The problem is that if your partner is going to explore her sexual potential, she will do it only with your encouragement and support, and she can't change if she knows that you are impatiently expecting her to hurry up. Have you noticed any of the changes she has been able to make? Have you let her know how proud you are of her because she is trying to do something about your sexual relationship?

Remember, you are the lucky one. You *do* feel the pleasure of frequent sexual arousal. Think about it from your partner's point of view. Everything she reads in novels and sees in movies tells her she should be experiencing hot passion that overwhelms the senses, but what does she feel? Nothing! Maybe she occasionally has some vague stirrings, and maybe she can eventually get turned on if the right things happen, but don't you think she would like to be as easily turned on as you are, and as often?

At the present time, I would guess that your partner wishes she never had to think about sex again—she really could live without it. Yet you can feel interested without giving it much thought. Your partner has to reprogram her mind and body to be able to experience even a small amount of what you take for granted. So, are you going to give her encouragement every step of the way, or are you going to criticize from the sidelines?

IDENTIFY YOUR KEY ISSUES

Go back over your notes and see if you can identify the issues that are most relevant to your particular situation. What have you found out about yourself? What points need to be discussed with your partner? Then go back and read through chapter 9 and see if you can predict her responses to the issues.

CHAPTER 11

DEVELOPING YOUR SEXUAL RELATIONSHIP

NOW THAT YOU'VE BOTH HAD THE OPPORTUNITY to think about your sexual relationship from an individual point of view, the task ahead of you is to bring it together as a couple. This process begins with the two of you discussing what you have discovered so far and how you each now see what has been happening in your sex life.

UNDERSTANDING THE SITUATION

The very first issue to clarify is why—or even if—your current situation is a problem. What do you each think her lack of interest in sex means? What's the most distressing thing about how things are? Are you worried that it means you don't love each other, that you are each somehow letting the other partner down, or that you are inadequate sexually? In talking these issues through, you may find that the only problem you have is that you haven't had the confidence to talk about them before; it may turn out that you are actually both quite happy with each other and content with your sexual relationship as it is now.

Simply understanding the situation more clearly may significantly increase your enjoyment of your sexual relationship, even if sexual frequency doesn't increase. Once the woman stops feeling abnormal and apologetic, and the man stops feeling hurt and rejected, two of the major impediments to a healthy, give-and-take sexual relationship have been dismantled. Despite individual differences, the partners can feel more connected as a couple, and their sex life can begin to take on new meaning. If your situation isn't as straightforward as that, however, it will take a little more time and energy to sort things out.

Start Talking

If you find it difficult to discuss what you have discovered so far, use this book as a workbook. Each of you can go back to the beginning and, with different-colored pens, mark what you consider the relevant points that should be discussed. When you've each done that, set aside some time and use the highlighted sections as a basis for discussion.

Can you reach agreement about the factors that have contributed to the worries you have about your sex life? Do you feel that now that you have a better understanding of individual and gender differences, you can accept the dissimilarities between you and build on what you share? Is your relationship basically fine, but your sex life is being put under pressure by an exhausting and demanding lifestyle? Are there some serious relationship issues that should be addressed? All of this needs to be discussed repeatedly until you reach some sort of mutual understanding about what's going on and have an idea of what you can do about it.

Resolving all the issues affecting your sexual relationship may be painful, but you need to be able to listen to each other's point of view, consider it, and genuinely try to find solutions rather than being defensive. The best way to achieve this is to start with the assumption that you are both right, just different, and each of you is really very curious about what makes your partner tick sexually. Neither of you should be making judgments about the other or imposing a set of expectations on the other. Good sex begins with mutual respect and goodwill.

AIMING FOR HASSLE-FREE SEX

One of the issues to reach agreement on is what "success" is. It may sound bizarre, but otherwise, how will you know when you are having a good time? You have two choices about what you consider to be success: (1) frequency of intercourse, type of sexual activity, and who initiates what and how often, or (2) more understanding and consideration of each other, irrespective of what you are actually doing.

The idea of relationship sex is to take the hassle out of sex. Sure, things would be easier if you were more similar in your levels of physical sex drive and were turned on by the same things, but hey, that's life. In a world where some people don't have adequate food and shelter, others cope with serious illness and disability, and some have suffered terrible misfortune, you two are really very lucky. You have each other, and that can be a very satisfying basis for your sexual relationship.

In a couple that shares mutual respect and goodwill, the woman isn't judged to be frigid because she doesn't experience any great urgency for sex, and the man isn't a sex maniac because sex is the best hobby he can think of. In a relationship characterized by hassle-free sex, each has a fond and easygoing tolerance of the differences between them, and potential conflict is dealt with in a gentle and humorous manner.

Because the partners live in the real world, they accept that the quality of sex ebbs and flows with the stresses of everyday life and that while there may be some disappointment that some sexual fantasies never materialize, there really is very little that happens in the sexual arena that causes major drama. If she doesn't feel like having sex, she can confidently tell him how she feels, and he can accept a gentle cuddle instead, or else she can go along with sex for the pleasure of being close. She may remain quiet and still, or she may unexpectedly become aroused. The point is that the couple enjoys what is possible, with few regrets about what may be missing.

Many couples find that accepting the concept of relationship sex leads to an increase in self-confidence and greater emotional closeness.

The lack of stress and the pleasure of accepting and being accepted more than make up for the absence of some of the physical thrills you may have read about in sex manuals.

Begin with Non-Demand Sex

Some of you will find that the relief of discovering that you aren't abnormal or inadequate and that there a lot of people out there who feel the same way you do is enough to boost your confidence and jump-start your sex life. Others will be at a loss to know how to get past the stalemate that has reduced your sex life to almost zero. This is particularly true for women who have struggled with their concerns about low libido for so long that the whole sex thing seems far too difficult to contemplate.

Let's start with a simple positive: You are reading this book, so you have at least a small amount of energy and some willingness to build a sexual relationship with your partner. If you are in the fortunate position of knowing that once you agree to participate in sex, you usually enjoy it and can even be aroused and come to orgasm, you can move on to the next section and discover the triggers that will help you say yes to sex.

If you find that sex is usually boring, tedious, or irritating, it's obviously a little more difficult for you to see it as a reasonable activity that you may have even a slight amount of interest in. Solving this puzzle is a little bit like unraveling a severely tangled ball of wool: First, you have to find one end, then slowly work your way through all the knots and tangles until the strands are free. For the woman who doesn't feel like having sex and gets very little out of it when she does engage in it, unraveling the problem begins with finding out how to change what happens during sex so that it's *less* boring, tedious, or irritating rather than hoping to make it pleasurable in the short term. Because there is no magic technique to make sex instantly pleasurable and dramatically increase sex drive, you need to experiment with different options during initiation, foreplay, and sex until you find out what helps.

These options are not likely to be anything like the hints you read in sex manuals, such as covering your body with whipped cream and allowing your partner to lick it off. Most low-drive women would probably see this as a quick way to mess up the sheets rather than anything that could be remotely pleasurable. Think about all you have read so far about individual and gender differences and the importance of the emotional and sensual aspects of affection and sex. Ideas for foreplay, such as being left alone to relax for a while once the children are in bed, a soft back massage, gentle tickling, or having your hair brushed, and low-key options for intercourse, such as gentle penetration using a lubricant, are all more likely to improve sex for women with low drive and lack of enjoyment.

With non-demand sex, the idea is that the woman tries to identify the aspects of sex that seem to cause the most obstacles. In chapter 9, I asked you to try to work out what would make sex more appealing. Did you come up with any ideas? If you're stuck, try to complete the sentence, "Sex would be better if . . ." Write down as many ideas as possible and keep coming back to add to the list. It doesn't matter if you come up with "Sex would be better if he only approached me once a week, or on Sundays, or not on Sundays, or not when he can see I'm busy," or you want him not to rush things, or you want absolutely no caressing of the breasts or kissing, or you want sex to be over more quickly or to last longer. Only by being completely honest about how you feel, and making any changes that will make sex less unpleasant, will you be able to move on to discovering what will make sex enjoyable and lessen your resistance to it.

The most important part of this process is listening to your body and trusting your own sense of what is right for you. If you feel or think something, it must be valid for you. If you tell yourself you are being stupid or that these thoughts and feelings are proof that you have a problem, you will go around in circles. Instead, take your time and work out what you can learn from these experiences. You can develop your sexual potential only from a positive base, so if you remain curious about your individual sexuality and start with even small changes that help you feel more comfortable with it, you have a better chance of building an enjoyable and satisfying sexual relationship.

The value of brief sex, or quickies, needs to be recognized. It seems crazy that we early sex therapists spent the 1970s trying to teach men that women need more foreplay instead of the traditional "wham-bam" sex and that we put pressure on them to learn to delay ejaculation, because now some women are pleading for less foreplay and brief intercourse. The fact is, sometimes the simple things in life can be rewarding. Quickies can be either fast and furious because both partners are keen for an easy orgasm, or fast and affectionate if emotional needs are the priority, but either way, they can fill an important need.

Brief sex can seem second-best if you tell your partner to hurry up and get it over and done with. A more intimacy-enhancing approach is to talk positively about quick sex, as in "I'm not feeling sexy, but cuddly sex would be nice." By talking about the issue now, you can both recognize what cuddly sex means without having to spell it out every time. You can develop body language signals, such as a gentle pat on the backside, to let your partner know you've had enough of foreplay and want to move on to intercourse, or you can tell him softly that you aren't really into it, which conveys that you are ready for him to ejaculate. Afterward, let him know that it felt nice to be close and you appreciated the brief episode, because he may worry that he has been using you and feel guilty about not making more effort for you.

Your partner has to be open to supporting you in whatever you try and, at least in the early stages of my approach, be prepared to give control of sex to you. This is the meaning of non-demand sex: There are no demands at all placed on the woman—she is given complete freedom to work things out at her own pace and in her own way. Her partner can let her know when he is interested in sex, and he can try some of the things he might like or that he thinks may help, but the woman is able to say no to any of these without recriminations or tension.

Some men balk at this. They may see this approach as being biased against their sexual needs, but as I asked before, what do you gain by pressuring your partner into complying with your sexual wishes when it's actually a negative experience for her? All you're doing is making the problem worse. It's a question of short-term losses for long-term gains: Patience and understanding now may reap great rewards for the coming years, but insisting on immediate sexual satisfaction can hasten the deterioration of your relationship.

More commonly, men express the fear that if they don't use some pressure, their partner will simply stop trying, and he will have no hope of ever having a satisfactory sex life. I can't guarantee that this won't happen, but this is why I emphasize the importance of your emotional relationship. Talking to, loving, and supporting each other helps to develop give-and-take compromises because you each genuinely want to please the other.

Using Triggers to Make It Easier to Say Yes to Sex

If you don't have a physical urge to have sex, what other triggers can you use to enhance sexual interest? We know that sex drive is a complicated phenomenon that is influenced by a variety of factors. Certainly, physical factors such as hormones play a part, as many women who experience changes in sex drive during their menstrual cycles will attest. But other factors are just as important: Your attitudes toward sex and the way you talk to yourself about it, receiving the right sensual stimulation, being in a receptive emotional state, and being in an environment that's conducive to sexual enjoyment. At any one time, any or all of these factors can be utilized to pique sexual interest without necessarily leading to spontaneous passion, and one of these influences may override others on occasion. The trick is to recognize and build on these triggers rather than waiting around for a physical buzz that may never happen.

Find Your Sensory Triggers

I've already discussed appropriate forms of sensual stimulation that women are more likely to enjoy than the breast and genital stimulation routinely portrayed in erotic movies. It makes sense that a woman is more likely to respond to attempts at sexual initiation if she receives the sensory experiences (which include touch, sight, smell, sound, and maybe even taste) that please her, no matter how routine or unusual her individual preferences may be. But a woman's willingness to have sex is determined partly by the mood she's in before sex is even thought of, so sensory triggers that may predispose you to think about sex also include things that help you unwind from daily stresses.

A lot of women tell me they have no idea what they like, so they can't begin to talk to their partner about it. Earlier, I asked you to think about what might make sex less annoying or tedious, and an important part of this process was to listen to your body and trust your instincts. Now I want to expand this exercise so that you consider any sensual experience that helps you feel relaxed, peaceful, and kindly disposed toward your partner. The most obvious are things like lying together in front of the fire on a cold winter's night (after you've put the kids to bed and turned the television off), having a relaxing bath or shower, sitting together on the floor on comfortable pillows, lying in bed and chatting quietly, or going for a walk on the beach or in a park. Activities such as these need to happen on a regular basis to produce a general feeling of relaxation and connection to your partner. Without these types of experiences, you may find it difficult to maintain a regular feeling of intimacy with your partner that helps promote sexual desire.

Some sensory triggers that may sometimes lead directly to sex could be having your back tickled while you are watching television, having your hair brushed or your feet massaged, or just idly stroking each other while you lie together on the sofa or bed. Sharing a special meal or treat, such as strawberries and ice cream with champagne, while lounging comfortably on cushions on the floor can whet the appetite for other things as well.

A more intimate exercise is showering or bathing together (if you like to share this activity; not everyone does), then drying each other gently. After that, try touching each other as if this were the first time you were ever naked together. Slowly run your fingertips over your partner's entire body and be interested in the textures and shapes you encounter. You can both be standing when you start but progress to lying down as you become more involved.

These are examples for you to think about. If none of them appeals to you, try to identify anything at all that you find soothing that might help you find it easier to appreciate sex with your partner. Then give him some ideas. Perhaps certain types of music help you get in the mood, either because that particular music stirs your emotions or because it helps distract you from your everyday thoughts. You may know that aromatherapy helps you relax and that candles provide a sensual atmosphere, so pass that on to your partner. You probably won't want the same thing every time, and your partner can't read your mind, so it will help both of you if you're able to let him know whenever you think of something that will help.

Your partner's role in this is to understand that you need sensory triggers such as these to help you even begin to be in the mood for sex and that without them, you are likely to find sexual touch annoying and prefer to avoid it.

Use Positive Self-Talk

The stream of thoughts that runs through your mind in any situation is called self-talk. In essence, your individual belief system and your thinking style influence the way you cope with life. In recent years, there has been a great deal of research into the relationship between the way people think and a variety of problems, such as depression, anxiety, low self-esteem, and anger.

A simple example of the power of self-talk is to think about how you usually cope in a traffic jam. Do you usually talk to yourself along the lines of, "This is terrible; I'm going to be late. Who is the idiot holding me up? What will I do if I get to my appointment late? I've had a rotten day, and now it's getting worse . . ." and so on; you get the idea. How would you expect to feel when you wind yourself up this way?

The alternative is a more rational form of self-talk: "It certainly is a nuisance that I'm being held up, but there's nothing I can do about it. If I'm late for my appointment, so be it; I'll deal with it somehow." With this type of self-talk, your stress levels remain reasonable, and while things may not work out as you might wish, how big is the problem in reality? If you think of the worst possible thing that could happen to you—perhaps one of your children becoming seriously ill—and call that 10 on a scale of zero to 10—how serious is a brief traffic jam? It's not even a 1, so why are you reacting to it as if it were a 5 or a 6, or more?

You can apply the same process to your low sex drive. When you know your partner is interested in sex, do you usually set off a train of self-talk along the lines of, "Oh, no, not that again. I really can't be bothered. Can't he see I'm not interested? Why does he need sex, anyway? What's wrong with me that I don't want it? There he goes again, touching my breasts, and I've told him so many times it's annoying. I suppose it's easier just to get it over and done with."

The alternative could be, "Hmm, he wants it again, and I don't really feel like it, but maybe it could be okay. The kids are asleep, it isn't too late, and maybe a quickie would be all right. I know he loves me so much and only wants to please me. His body feels nice, comforting. I need to slow him down, just hold me—yes, that's better. It's nice to be alone with him for a while."

Women who can respond sexually once things get going obviously can have even more optimistic self-talk. "He's interested again, but I really would rather go to sleep. On the other hand, if we spend a bit of time unwinding, I know I can get turned on, and an orgasm would be good, so why not?"

Take some time to recognize your negative self-talk. If you identify attitudes such as, "This whole thing makes me sick!" or "Why should I give it to him?" it may be time to see a relationship counselor. On the other hand, if your self-talk is more along the lines of, "I can't really be bothered" or "It's so irritating," then working on communication with your partner, changing foreplay so it's more appropriate to your needs, and developing more positive, realistic self-talk can make quite a difference.

Focus on Your Emotional Triggers

In the same way that using positive self-talk can help you to choose to have sex, focusing on the emotional positives of a sexual encounter can make it easier to look forward to sex. Because many couples with differences in sexual desire have good emotional relationships, this can help them focus on the emotional bond as a good reason to have sex instead of worrying about behavioral goals, such as arousal and orgasm or different techniques and positions. Think about sex as a time to reconnect with the man you're sharing your life with. Anticipate that during sex, you can let yourself sink into the feelings of love, joy, security, and acceptance and express how you feel with touch that communicates your love and caring to your partner. Imagine running your hands along his body and enjoying the feel of his skin, smiling at each other, stroking each other, whatever—this man is your life partner, and connecting with him emotionally in this way makes the daily hassles a lot easier to cope with.

Thus, combining your feelings with optimistic self-talk would go something like this: "I know he's interested, but I don't know that I'm that energetic. But then, when I look at him, he really is sweet, and he does so much for me, he loves me very much, and I feel so safe with him, it would be nice to feel close to him, to feel good."

Getting in touch with the emotional bond between you and your partner can be a strong cue that will help you want to be intimate. Even so, there will be times when you're unable to get yourself interested in sex no matter what you do, and if you are stressed out from the day or aren't feeling that close, it's reasonable to forgo sex.

Take Advantage of Environmental Triggers

The right environment can definitely make a difference sometimes, particularly for women. Men seem to be more able to switch off the distractions of an unsettled child or neighbors talking just outside the bedroom window. Generally speaking, women, particularly those with low desire, are more likely to want a comfortable, private environment with no chance of outside distraction.

The classic scene in the movies is a couple on an empty beach, making love as the waves wash gently over their bodies. However, whenever I see a scene like that, I can't help thinking (1) they must be cold, (2) the sand must be getting in some strange places, (3) they are probably being eaten alive by sand flies, and (4) what are they going to dry themselves with afterward?

It makes sense for you to take the setting for sex into consideration. Your partner is probably setting himself up for rejection if he approaches you while your toddler is napping and could wake up at any minute or you are vacationing in a cabin with two teenage children, or if he wants you to have sex on the narrow, cold bench in the bathroom.

Just to emphasize the point, however, that sexuality is expressed differently among different people, I once counseled a woman who enjoyed sex more in unusual places away from home because she felt she had left the daily hassles behind. Other women have fond memories of their sexual experiences in cars. Make sure this item comes up for discussion so you and your partner are each aware of your preferences; it would be a shame to spend so much time on this issue only to overlook the obvious.

Maximizing each of these influences—the right sensory stimulation, optimistic self-talk, the emotional bond between you, and the right environment—can make it a lot easier to respond to your partner's advances.

ALTERNATIVES TO INTERCOURSE

Of course, in cases where there are marked discrepancies in sexual desire between the couple, there are going to be occasions when one partner is highly aroused, and the other has no hope of raising even mild interest no matter what triggers are used.

The most obvious alternative to intercourse is self-stimulation, usually called masturbation. Despite endless articles in magazines extolling the benefits of masturbation, attitudes still vary widely. Some men didn't feel comfortable with masturbation as teenagers and don't feel any better about it now. Other men believe that they shouldn't have to masturbate once they are married and are quite put off by the idea.

There are men who are quite happy to masturbate when their partner isn't interested in sex, but their partner is horrified at the thought of it. I have counseled couples in which the woman has discovered the man masturbating, and this has set off a major argument. Sometimes the woman interprets his masturbation as a form of sexual perversion.

Often, however, masturbation represents a simple solution to a common problem, and I would encourage you to discuss it as an alternative to intercourse. The man can masturbate in privacy in the bathroom or bedroom, but it can be infinitely more satisfying for him if the woman can give him support by resting her head on his shoulder or caressing his chest, tickling his thighs, or whatever feels nice while he brings himself to orgasm. In this way, she acknowledges that she is with him in spirit, if not in body. I know a lot of men aren't comfortable stimulating themselves in the presence of their partner, and some women don't want this type of involvement, so this may never be an option for you. However, in the interests of equality, the idea of a woman touching herself is a turn-on for many men and is now accepted as a normal part of sexual activity between a man and a woman, so perhaps reversing the roles isn't such a huge leap.

A similar alternative is for the woman to bring her partner to orgasm by hand, and lots of couples have practiced this option for years. It's fine if the woman isn't feeling too tired, but otherwise, it can be not only a pain in the neck, so to speak, but also a pain in the hand, arm, shoulder, and back. Bringing someone to orgasm by hand, while pleasurable for the receiver, is often hard work for the giver, but if you're not too tired and have your sense of humor intact, it can be a lot of fun. Just make sure you're in a comfortable position before you begin.

You may also be happy to perform oral sex on your partner when you don't feel interested in anything for yourself. If you don't find this acceptable, though, don't feel there is something wrong with you. A lot of women don't like the thought of oral sex, and this is merely an issue of individual differences rather than a sign of inhibition or inadequacy. You may be more comfortable with a shared option, such as using your mouth to stimulate his penis for a while, then having him bring himself to orgasm with his hand as you continue to kiss him on the base of his penis or his thighs.

Another alternative is mutual stimulation, which is pleasant on those lazy occasions when you both feel an orgasm would be nice, but one or both of you can't be bothered with doing too much work. The position I suggest is that you both lie on your backs side by side, with each partner's feet next to the other's head. Then put your nearest arm underneath his nearest leg, which is raised slightly, while he does the same to you. This position gives you comfortable, easy access to each other's genitals. It's also convenient if you don't feel like having an orgasm; you can lie there and daydream quite comfortably while your partner enjoys the stimulation.

It's also worthwhile to consider acquiring a vibrator. The best type isn't a penis-shaped one but rather a body massager that has a flat rubber pad for massaging the face; they are available in the appliance departments of most major stores. A vibrator is useful for helping a woman achieve orgasm, but it can also be enjoyable for a man. He can use it by himself, or his partner can do it with him. Experiment with different techniques. Men tell me they like stimulation between their legs behind the penis (be careful near the testicles), as well as on the shaft and head.

If the vibration is uncomfortable or too strong, put one hand over his penis and use the vibrator on top; this will produce gentler stimulation.

If none of these alternatives is acceptable in your relationship, then frankly, the man's option is either cold showers or developing the ability to ignore the frustration until it goes away.

WHAT HAPPENS IF THINGS DON'T CHANGE?

Suppose that in 12 months' time, things are pretty much the same as they are now—what would you do? Would the situation be sufficiently serious to warrant ending the relationship? If so, does that mean there is so much tension between you now that you really can't give any attempts to improve the situation a fair try? Differences in sexual desire often lead to divorce. What are you each prepared to do to make sure that doesn't happen to you? What do you each need the other to understand, and what do you each want to say to the other, to try to avoid this outcome?

Perhaps if you don't believe that you can work as a team on this issue, if both of you aren't prepared to contribute to change or you believe that you truly are incompatible, it may be more honest and in the end less painful to consider ending the relationship now.

If, on the other hand, you say that you would stay together even if things didn't change, you are telling each other that there are enough strengths in your relationship to compensate for the sexual difficulties— and perhaps that's not such a bad thing to discover!

CHAPTER 12

STRENGTHENING YOUR EMOTIONAL RELATIONSHIP

WHEN I RUN WORKSHOPS ON SEXUALITY, I always have an introductory session on past sexual beliefs and practices, using examples from old texts as I did in chapter 1. These usually bring a laugh or a gasp from those present, because some of the things people believed and did, even 50 years ago, can now seem quaint or bizarre. Were some couples really so ignorant that they didn't know what to do on their wedding night? How could women not know about the clitoris or have any idea about orgasm? Is it possible that couples accepted a few minutes of foreplay as good sex? Was a woman really expected to follow her husband's lead and have no needs of her own?

The point, of course, is to demonstrate that what we believe about sex and what we accept as normal and reasonable are entirely dependent on the society and the time in history we happen to be born into. By the end of the exercise, most people have reached the logical conclusion that if past beliefs and practices can be challenged, the same must be true for what we do and believe today. Since it's highly unlikely that we just happen to be living in the perfect moment in time when we have all the definitive answers about sex, the inescapable conclusion is that in another 50 years, some of what we currently believe and do sexually will seem laughable or odd to that generation.

What will our grandchildren point to in amazement when they read some of the popular books on sex from this time? Which of the beliefs we hold so dear will they discuss among themselves with a tinge of pity in their voices? What areas of ignorance will future sex researchers uncover that will make us seem naive?

The irony is that no matter what future generations choose to question, or what values and behaviors they accept as entirely normal and reasonable for themselves, all of that will be challenged by *their* grandchildren, and the concept of normal sexuality will be reinvented yet again.

There is a way of getting around the problem of trying to decide what a normal person should be capable of sexually and how to help someone who isn't achieving this. Think about the main reason that people consult sex therapists. What is worrying you the most about your low libido? Why is your partner so distressed about your lack of interest in sex? In the majority of cases I see, although there is certainly a hope that enjoyment of the physical aspects of sex can be improved, the primary motivation for a couple to seek help is to improve their relationship. The question to ask then is, Can this need be met in some other way? For many couples, the answer is yes; what they want more than anything is more relaxed and easy intimacy, and this isn't tied just to sex. It means that strengthening other areas of the relationship can produce a win-win outcome. It may not matter if the specific sexual behaviors don't change if you feel closer in other ways, and a bonus may be that enhancing your intimate emotional relationship can trigger changes in your sexual relationship.

RECOGNIZE WHAT'S RIGHT, NOT JUST WHAT'S WRONG

When a couple is having a significant problem of any kind, it can feel overwhelming. They may disagree about sex, money, childrearing, each other's family, or any of a number of other issues. They may talk about the problem a lot, they may think about it even when they're getting on with other things, and they may sometimes argue about it. Eventually, they may feel as if it dominates the relationship.

When a couple is worried about their sexual relationship, it's under-standable that they may question the quality of their emotional relation-ship. They may have had numerous fruitless, hurtful, and sometimes heated discussions about their sexual differences, making it easy to lose sight of the many things they are doing right for each other on a day-to-day basis. Yet, as I have said, the majority of couples in this situation nevertheless have a sound emotional relationship in many ways, and they underestimate the strengths that have brought them this far.

This suggests an important starting point for restoring harmony to your relationship. You have already decided that there are good reasons for you to stay with your partner and work through the sexual issues that seem to be swamping your relationship. Think about these reasons. They may seem ordinary, such as staying to provide a family life for your chil-dren or to preserve financial security. Reasons for being in a relationship vary from person to person, as do the wants and needs an individual brings to it. While romantic love is a wonderful concept, it's not neces-sary for a relationship to work, as the success of many arranged marriages demonstrates. What is important is that there are reasons that are mean-ingful enough for you to feel that staying with your partner is a better option than leaving. Having decided to stay, however, it would make sense for both of you to be willing to put some energy into making your relationship as mutually satisfying and enjoyable as possible.

Once a couple realizes that they do want to stay together, I encourage them to identify what it is that they do right together. Taking time to reflect on what works in your relationship, what the good parts are, helps to restore your confidence in it as well as your appreciation of each other.

If you both drew a pie chart representing how much is good between you and how much of the relationship is a problem, what would you end up with? Are most areas of your relationship solid despite the sexual wor-ries? What would you say are the strengths between you—what works? Do you share childcare responsibilities, work out your finances without hassles, or help each other out in various other ways? Can you talk over problems together without tension and conflict?

If you estimate that more than 75 percent of your relationship is good, you're doing okay. If you rate 90 percent as satisfying, you can really afford to smile!

The other basic way to help you appreciate what's right between you is to identify what you like about each other. I tend to think that liking each other is as important as being in love; certainly, many couples who have enjoyed their relationships over decades say that being good friends has been the cornerstone of their happiness together. Psychologist John Gottman, Ph.D., has spent 30 years researching what makes a satisfying relationship, and he came to the same conclusion: The happiest couples were those who had a deep friendship. They enjoyed each other's company, knew each other very well, accommodated each other's likes and dislikes, accepted any personal quirks, and were interested in each other's well-being.

What first attracted you to your partner? Do you share a sense of humor? Do you have the same life values and similar goals? Do you admire your partner's work ethic, compassion, or spiritual commitment? Is your partner honest and trustworthy, and can you depend on him in times of crisis? If you met your partner now, would you still want to get to know him? What would you miss if your relationship ended?

This isn't to say that you like everything about each other. You each may have characteristics that your partner finds annoying, disappointing, or even hurtful, and these may need to be explored to see whether they can be modified in any way. But, as we all know, no one is perfect, so the bottom line is whether you feel that you have chosen a good person to be your life partner. If you know you have, then building a strong emotional relationship starts with letting each other know the good things you're thinking and feeling about each other and your life together.

Say What's Right

While specific problems, such as differences in libido, disagreements about childrearing practices, and arguments about financial issues, can all take their toll, one of the most destructive forces that can bring down a relationship is the way the partners talk to each other in their daily lives. In our society, we seem to have a major problem in that we find it very easy to criticize and hard to praise. It doesn't help that the trend in the media, whether in tough cop movies or family comedies, is to showcase smart wisecracks that are often cruel and demeaning.

The pattern of negative communication starts with parents and children. Some parents always seem to notice when their children do something wrong but often forget to comment when they do the right thing. If they praise their kids, it's often for some specific achievement, such as doing well in school. What children need from Mom and Dad is unconditional love and spontaneous expressions of that love. Offering a child smiles, hugs, kisses, and genuine praise just because he *is* teaches him that he is worthwhile and lovable. Certainly, children need realistic criticism and discipline, but overall, they need more positive rather than negative communication from their parents.

Without such regular reassurance, children may grow up believing themselves to be inadequate and unlovable, because they've learned to recognize only their apparent faults, not their good qualities. They may carry this negative, pessimistic communication pattern into adulthood, causing a catastrophic impact on relationships that are meant to be intimate and loving.

If feelings of intimacy, acceptance, and support seem to be missing from your relationship, think about how you communicate with each other. Do you find it easy to express negative feelings, such as irritation, frustration, annoyance, and anger, but difficult to offer positive feelings, such as love, concern, approval, consideration, and respect? Is it easy to say "You're late!" but hard to say "I'm glad you're home"? Do you criticize, as in, "You haven't taken the trash out/mowed the lawn/tidied up/cooked dinner," but forget to say, "Thanks, Love," "You've done a good job," "Great meal," and so on? How often do you say "I love you," "I'm glad I'm married to you," "You are still the best-looking man/woman in town," or "That was a lovely evening, Darling"? When was the last time you smiled at each other, shared a joke together, or had a good laugh?

Rather than being confined to the honeymoon stage of a relationship, this positive side of communication becomes more important the longer you stay together. Some tension and conflict are inevitable in any relationship, and the warm feelings generated by happy, positive communication act as a buffer against the effects of angry words or irritated comments. Studies have shown that successful, long-lasting marriages are generally characterized by significantly more positive communication than negative.

Even without major disagreements, if you never say anything nice to each other, it's difficult to develop an atmosphere of intimacy. Where is that special bond that makes you feel like a couple instead of two people who share a house and occasionally have sex? It's easy to forget how much you mean to each other if you rarely express your feelings.

If you don't feel close and companionable on a day-to-day basis, this is highly likely to interfere with how comfortable and relaxed you are when you're having sex. If you've spent the evening picking on each other, you'll hardly be in the mood to appreciate the joy of being together. And if you carry your pattern of negative communication into your sex life, it shouldn't come as a surprise if sex lacks the sense of emotional connection and enjoyment you're seeking. For example, comments such as "Leave me alone," "I don't like that," "You're frigid," "You're a sex maniac," "Do you have to just lie there?" and "Hurry up, can't you?" are unlikely to promote sexual desire and pleasure. On the other hand, comments such as "I like it when you rub my back," "It feels good to lie quietly like this," and "Your skin feels nice against mine" are much more likely to encourage a desire for physical intimacy.

If you can find absolutely nothing positive to comment on about any aspect of your relationship or each other, there's more to your problem than just communication style. However, in most relationships, there are at least some things that are appreciated, respected, and enjoyed, and they all need to be acknowledged. If you have just realized that your relationship is dominated by a negative pattern of communication, don't despair. It's possible to change your communication style slowly and thus develop a more harmonious and intimate relationship. The catch is that you have to say what is genuine, that is, to recognize good feelings that are there but aren't being expressed. It doesn't work in the long term merely to play at saying good things; it's too difficult to keep making up new things you feel you should be saying.

The easiest way to make the switch from negative to positive communication is to begin by telling your partner the answers to the earlier question, "Why do you want to stay in this relationship?" Then talk about what each of you has each identified as the aspects of your relationship that work well and the qualities of your partner that you like and respect. After that, the aim is to recognize any good thoughts and feelings you have toward your partner and learn to express them as easily as you criticize, complain, or withdraw. If you're pleased to be home, say so. If you appreciate something your partner does, no matter how small, be sure you comment on it. If you feel any warm or happy feelings about your partner, pass them on.

Surprisingly, even if your partner isn't consciously participating in this rebuilding of your emotional life, if you make the move into more positive territory, it's likely that in time, he'll follow your lead. You know how nice it feels when someone makes you feel wanted, needed, and cared for. This is how you can make your partner feel, and eventually, he should respond to that. Don't give up. Even if it seems like slow going, it's worth it to persevere. Even if in the end your partner's behavior doesn't change, you will have at least benefited by developing a more optimistic approach toward relationships.

MAKE TIME FOR EACH OTHER

I have a theory that many of today's relationship breakdowns can be blamed on television. Okay, bear with me; I know this sounds frivolous, and I'm not being entirely serious, but there is some sense to this idea. How much time do you and/or your partner spend in front of the TV? Do you talk to each other while you're watching? Most couples have only limited conversations, even if they're watching something that is barely interesting. Yet talking over the events of the day, engaging in general chit-chat, is an important building block in an intimate and caring relationship. For one thing, being able to chat makes it easier to get into more serious levels of conversation. If the only time you talk to each other is when you need to discuss serious issues, the relationship can seem burdened by problems. Watching television inhibits casual, friendly conversation, and ultimately this will affect how close and comfortable you feel with each other.

Television also directly affects your sexual enjoyment because it means that sex is often left until the last thing, late at night. We find it hard to pass up our favorite shows, and watching TV is such an accepted part of everyday life now that we fail to recognize that we're putting the latest sitcom or a football game ahead of our relationships. Postponing sex until after we've finished watching means that it happens at the worst possible time—when we're tired. And there's another downside to TV: The unrealistic views we have of sex and relationships are reinforced by many of the shows we watch.

Of course, the lack of companionable intimacy is the result of more than merely watching too much TV. We live in a hectic, 24/7 society, with couples sometimes working opposing shifts, and there's not always a definite time set aside for relaxing or socializing. In previous generations, society closed down at the end of the day, and couples had time (without the distraction of TV) to unwind together. For some couples then, sex was their entertainment, not an afterthought, and without the pressure to get it right and include sophisticated techniques, sex was an easy way to maintain emotional connection.

In today's busy lifestyle, it may take thought to make sure you get time together. What did you do in the early stages of your relationship, when you were getting to know each other? Can you make sure you go to the movies or have a picnic or go for a walk most weeks? Maybe you could set aside one evening a week when you put the kids to bed early or hire a babysitter so that you can have some down time together. Even preparing the evening meal together can give you some time to catch up with each other. For some couples, going to bed at the same time and making sure they have time to chat before settling down for the night keeps them in touch.

A relationship that has little time invested in it is like a flower without water: It will shrivel up and fade away. Only you can decide whether time together is a priority and then make it happen.

BE REALISTIC ABOUT ARGUMENTS

If we were all perfect superhumans who never made mistakes, were never unreasonable, and were never in a rotten mood, we could handle disagreements in a civilized manner and agree to disagree when we couldn't reach a compromise. We are, of course, imperfect, ordinary human beings, and some degree of tension, misunderstanding, or argument seems inevitable in most relationships. In a relationship that is basically sound, the occasional disagreement need not cause any long-lasting damage. Admittedly, after an argument, you may feel a little distant from your partner and perhaps be a little annoyed for a few days, but if your relationship is usually healthy and happy, you'll get over it.

The work of Dr. Gottman provides some important insight into resolving conflict in a healthy relationship. He found that the most successful couples are those whose relationships are characterized by mutual respect and willingness to listen to each other's point of view, even if they don't agree and never reach a compromise.

Interestingly, Dr. Gottman found that what couples actually do is less important than how they treat each other emotionally. For example, relationship counselors often recommend that a couple develop specific conflict-resolution strategies, such as using I-language rather than you-language. This simply means that when you're having a disagreement, you should describe the problem only from your point of view and avoid accusatory or inflammatory language, such as "You make me so angry!" He found that some couples could use all the wrong strategies from the experts' point of view and still resolve or live with their differences, provided they were able to convey through their tone of voice or other actions that they cared about what their partners felt and wanted.

Arguments are more of a problem when they are frequent and intense. Some couples say they argue about anything, and even small issues can lead to bitter exchanges. Are you arguing to hurt rather than having a frank exchange of opinions? Do you hit your partner with a barrage of words to force him into submission? Do you have any intention of listening to your partner, or are you only waiting for your chance to break in with your views? Are insults used as weapons to undermine each other? Are arguments about winning, so the person who gives way is seen as the loser? If this is the case, and you still feel the relationship is worth saving, you may benefit from developing more constructive conflict-resolution skills. You can learn to recognize the underlying dynamics that are sabotaging any attempts to settle disputes and develop healthier ways of addressing the issues. While strategies such as the use of I-language aren't the complete answer, they can help diffuse the emotional heat that some couples bring to any disagreement. Because arguments that become so hostile are highly destructive to a healthy, intimate relationship, it's important to work on changing this aspect of your interaction. You can find many books that address this problem in detail (see Recommended Reading), or you may prefer to consult a therapist who's skilled in this area. However, learning the art of fair fighting is not as important as building respect, tolerance, and goodwill in the relationship.

PRACTICE RESPECT, TOLERANCE, AND GOODWILL

While I agree with the traditional wisdom that a good marriage takes work, I sometimes think we make it harder than it needs to be. If we think about it in its simplest terms, the purpose of marriage is for two people to form a partnership to help each other get through life, so that the partners' lives are better when they're together than they would be if they were apart. The most successful partnerships seem to be based on good friendship characterized by shared values and similar life goals, where differences are respected and tolerated.

How hard can this be? What do we try to teach our children about how friends should treat each other? We expect even very young children to learn to share, to respect each other's toys, to not be bossy, to cooperate, and to not be mean. We want them to develop insight into their own behavior so that they can recognize when they've broken any of these simple rules, to take responsibility when they've done something hurtful to a friend, and to be strong enough to apologize. This means we want our kids to acquire empathy, that is, to be able to see things from other people's point of view and to understand the impact of their behavior on others. We try to teach them to be tolerant of others who are different in some way, and we want them to be generous, kind, and thoughtful. At the same time, we want them to be confident enough to stand up to bullies and assertive enough to reasonably express their own needs. The message at the core of all these lessons is that you must be a good friend to have a good friend.

If we believe that little children can learn all these things, how much easier should it be for adults? Yet, in many relationships I see that are in trouble, these simple values have become lost, as if we expect less of ourselves than we do of children. What I find refreshing is that when these values are rediscovered, the couple remembers why they want their children to learn them: It makes life so much easier.

In a good friendship, the friends respect each other's opinions, values, and actions even if they don't always entirely agree with them. If there are important differences, the friends can discuss them in ways that demonstrate this respect. They are willing to listen to each other's point of view and don't belittle each other when they can't reach agreement. If things get a little heated, they back off from the discussion rather than allow it to escalate to a damaging level. Because they respect each other, however, they don't waste energy nitpicking trivial issues, and they wisely avoid more sensitive subjects that they know can't be resolved.

Respect in a relationship acknowledges that life isn't black and white and that for one person to be right, the other doesn't have to be wrong. Recognizing this can help you avoid pointless stressful discussions and arguments. If you respect your partner in most ways, allow that to reduce the workload in your relationship by limiting your challenges to issues that are really important, not mere differences of opinion. Even in important matters such as childrearing, does it really matter if you do things differently? Showing respect for your partner builds feelings of acceptance and reassurance and makes the relationship lighter, which in turn makes it easier to be intimate.

Tolerance is a logical extension of respect. In most relationships, there are some things that cause irritation, annoyance, frustration, or even embarrassment. They can be simple, such as the way your partner squeezes the toothpaste tube or leaves the toilet seat up, or more serious, such as his tendency to be loud and tell weak jokes at parties. Tolerance in a relationship recognizes that sometimes you each do things that drive the other crazy, but unless there are serious consequences, you take a breath, let the irritation pass, and get on with it. The good thing about developing tolerance is that the benefits go both ways: You can each be yourselves without worrying that the other is going to take you to task. Eventually, the relationship becomes stronger because the give-and-take of tolerance can mean that irritation at some things eventually turns into a form of fondness for each other's idiosyncrasies, creating a gentler, kinder atmosphere.

From this basis, you're more likely to create a relationship founded on goodwill. Goodwill means that you want the best for each other, and you are prepared to put yourself out to help or please each other. You may be tired yourself, but if you see that your partner needs help, you make the effort to assist. You may not be really keen about going to a social function your partner is looking forward to, but you're happy to go and to make the time as enjoyable as possible for his sake. Your partner may receive a promotion at work or gain some recognition, and even though you may feel a little jealous or not really believe it's such a big deal, you genuinely delight in his happiness. You really do care that your partner has a cold, and you don't mind pampering him until he feels better.

The benefits of mutual goodwill are obvious. If you look out for each other and try to make each other's life less stressful and more enjoyable, your life together will become easier. Consider how good it feels to know that your partner will give you a hand when you need it, look after you when you're feeling down or sick, and share your good times with genuine delight. Think about how confident and worthwhile it makes you feel to know that you do the same for him. Relationships don't work well when there is competition over who is the most tired or puts in the most effort and there's resentment and reluctance to do anything for each other. When you're both committed to each other's welfare, you can see that it produces rewards that far outweigh the effort expended.

TAKE RESPONSIBILITY FOR CHANGE

For most of the 20th century, the model used in the treatment of psychological problems was based on the assumption that all the troubled person had to do was talk through his problem until he understood what it was and what had caused it. Insight therapy assumed that change would automatically follow this new awareness. However, research over the last decades of the century found that this approach rarely led to any significant improvement. Instead, the solution lies in using the new understanding to create ideas and strategies for change and in being motivated to put them into effect.

You began to read this book because either you or your partner was troubled by your low libido. The book has covered a wide range of strategies that can help you address that worry. I hope you have gained some understanding of the causes in your particular situation and have developed some ideas to tackle the issues that are causing distress to you both.

However, nothing will change unless you are both willing to take responsibility for doing things differently from now on. Toward the end of my sessions with clients, I focus on the importance of acting on the knowledge they have gained about themselves and their relationships. The first question I ask is, "What do you need your partner to do in the next few days and weeks that would let you know he is working on the issues that are important to you and would help you feel more loved and secure?" It can't be too big a step, because if it were that easy, say, for her to give him sex whenever he wanted it, they wouldn't need counseling in the first place. I want you to take the time now to talk this over with your partner or to write out the points you want to discuss at the appropriate time.

The next question is, "What are *you* prepared to do to let your partner know you are taking the issues seriously and are taking responsibility for improving the emotional and sexual relationship?" Again, either take the time to talk or jot down some ideas for later discussion.

Some people aren't prepared to take the last question seriously. One woman said she wasn't particularly interested in how the lack of sex was affecting her husband, and she had no intention of doing anything about it. Another man said that he didn't feel he had to change at all—his wife simply had to recognize how good she had it already and get her act together. Other people say that they don't see why they should change until their partners take the first step.

If this is also your attitude, take a moment to reflect on how you feel about the problems in your relationship. You may feel sad, lonely, inadequate, guilty, and frustrated and believe that your partner is the main cause of all your problems. The irony is that your partner is likely to feel exactly the same way. I am often amazed at how clearly the partners in a relationship mirror each other's feelings without realizing it.

Most of the couples I see are actually both feeling worried and inadequate, with each partner believing he or she is letting the other down, so in these cases, they take huge steps forward when they recognize that they share similar fears and need to reassure each other.

When you believe you haven't done anything to contribute to the problem, however, you may resent being told that you have to play a part in improving the situation—but this is unfortunately the case. Listen to what your partner is asking you to do so that he or she can feel more secure in the relationship, and this will give you the clue as to your role in solving the problem. Often, people have different priorities, so you may not believe that what your partner wants is important, but your act of respect, tolerance, and goodwill is to accept that what your partner is asking is significant.

Sometimes, couples get bogged down in believing that if they love each other, they shouldn't have to spell out what is needed. For example, the woman may be upset that she has to ask her partner to help with cooking dinner or looking after the children. "I shouldn't have to ask; surely he's an adult and can notice these things." Unfortunately, you may have to tell each other what you need and ask for help, year in and year out. Having to ask to have your needs met isn't a sign of a relationship in trouble—it's the willingness to try to meet each other's needs that is the issue. In this example, if the woman wants her partner to do more to help at home in order for her to feel that he's making an effort to care for her, the realistic question is whether he's prepared to pitch in when she lets him know she needs help.

When each partner is willing to listen to what the other wants and is prepared to make the effort to meet those needs, they both begin to feel more appreciated and secure in the relationship. When this happens, the healthy emotions that have been swamped by the tension between them start to emerge. And some people find the process simpler than they expected. Sometimes ancient wisdom is accurate after all: Treating others as you wish to be treated can yield benefits for the giver and the receiver.

GOOD LOVING OVER THE YEARS

Modern motivational speakers are fond of saying that if a person wants something badly enough and is prepared to work hard to achieve that goal, eventually he will get there. A moment's quiet reflection shows that this depends very much on the goals that you aim for. Not every athlete will win a gold medal, nor will every entrepreneur achieve great wealth. And even with the best will in the world, not everyone with low libido will develop a passionate sex drive.

How you deal with the wins and losses in your life is up to you, and to a large extent, this will depend on what you define as success and failure. An athlete can feel proud in the knowledge that he has done the absolute best he could do. An entrepreneur can achieve contentment knowing that she has invested wisely and attained the means to live comfortably. Living with low libido doesn't mean you have to miss out on good loving if the goal you set for yourself and strive to achieve is a relationship based on respect, tolerance, and goodwill. I hope the ideas discussed in this book will help you attain a relationship that sustains you and your partner into old age.

Recommended Reading

Cass, Vivienne. *The Elusive Orgasm*. Bentley, Australia: Brightfire Press, 2004.

Gottman, John M., and Nan Silver. *The Seven Principles for Making Marriage Work*. New York: Three Rivers, 1999.

Heiman, Julia, and Joseph LoPiccolo. *Becoming Orgasmic*. London: Piatkus Books, 1988.

Hendrix, Harville. *Getting the Love You Want*. London: Pocket Books, 2005.

Kaschak, Ellyn, and Leonore Tiefer, eds. *A New View of Women's Sexual Problems*. New York: Haworth, 2001.

McGraw, Phillip C. *Relationship Rescue*. New York: Hyperion, 2000.

McKay, Matthew, and Patrick Fanning. *Self-Esteem,* 3rd ed. Oakland: New Harbinger, 2000.

Seligman, Martin. *Learned Optimism*. New York: Free Press, 1998.

Bibliography

"The Agony Column," *Cosmopolitan* (Australian ed.), September 1996.

"Anatomical Relationship between Urethra and Clitoris," *Journal of Urology*, vol. 159, June 1998.

Bancroft, John. *Human Sexuality and Its Problems*, 2nd ed. London: Churchill Livingstone, 1989.

Berman, Jennifer, and Laura Berman. *For Women Only*. New York: Henry Holt, 2001.

Brauer, Alan P., and Donna Brauer. *Extended Sexual Orgasm*. Sydney: Horwitz Grahame, 1984.

Brecher, Edward. *The Sex Researchers*. London: Andre Deutsch, 1970.

Brecher, Edward, and Ruth Brecher. *An Analysis of Human Sexual Response*. New York: New American Library, 1966.

Brothers, Joyce. *Woman*. New York: MacFadden, 1962.

Comfort, Alex. *The Joy of Sex*. London: Quartet Books, 1973.

Crenshaw, Theresa. L. *Your Guide to Better Sex*. London: Book Club Associates, 1984.

Davis, Maxine. *Sexual Responsibility in Marriage*. London: Fontana, 1966.

———. *The Sexual Responsibility of Woman*. London: Fontana, 1964.

Davis, Michele W. *The Sex-Starved Marriage*. New York: Simon & Schuster, 2003.

Diamond, Milton. *Sex Watching*. London: Macdonald, 1984.

"Distress about Sex: A National Survey of Women in Heterosexual Relationships," *Archives of Sexual Behavior*, vol. 32, no. 3, June 2003.

"Female Androgen Deficiency Syndrome," *Medscape Women's Health*, vol. 6, no. 2, 2001. www.medscape.com/viewpublication/128_index.

"The Female Sexual Response: A Different Model," *Journal of Sex & Marital Therapy*, vol. 26, 2000.

Fisher, Helen. *Anatomy of Love*. New York: Fawcett Columbine, 1992.

Gottman, John M., and Nan Silver. *The Seven Principles for Making Marriage Work*. New York: Three Rivers, 1999.

Gray, John. *Mars and Venus in the Bedroom*. New York: HarperCollins, 1995.

———. *Men Are from Mars, Women Are from Venus*. New York: Harper-Collins, 1992.

Gregersen, Edgar. *Sexual Practices: The Story of Human Sexuality*. London: Book Club Associates, 1982.

Hilliard, Marion. *A Woman Doctor Looks at Love and Life*. Sydney: Family Life Movement of Australia, 1975.

Kaschak, Ellyn, and Leonore Tiefer, eds. *A New View of Women's Sexual Problems*. New York: Haworth, 2001.

Kassorla, Irene. *Nice Girls Do—And Now You Can Too*. New York: Granada, 1980.

Katchadourian, Herant A. *Fundamentals of Human Sexuality*, 4th ed. New York: Holt, Rinehart and Winston, 1985.

Kinsey, Alfred C., Wardell B. Pomeroy, and Clyde E. Martin. *Sexual Behavior in the Human Male*. Philadelphia: W. B. Saunders, 1948.

Kinsey, Alfred C. et al. *Sexual Behavior in the Human Female*. Philadelphia: W.B. Saunders, 1953.

Laumann, Edward O. et al. *The Social Organization of Sexuality: Sexual Practices in the United States*. Chicago: University of Chicago Press, 1994.

Leiblum, Sandra, and Judith Sachs. *Getting the Sex You Want*. New York: Crown, 2002.

"Life Satisfaction, Symptoms, and the Menopausal Transition," *Medscape Women's Health*, vol. 5, no. 4, 2000. www.medscape.com/viewpublication/128_index.

Marcus, Steven. *The Other Victorians*. London: Corgi, 1969.

Masters, William H., and Virginia E. Johnson. *Human Sexual Inadequacy*.

Boston: Little, Brown, 1970.

———. *Human Sexual Response*. Boston: Little, Brown, 1966.

Masters, William H., Virginia E. Johnson, and Robert C. Kolodny, *Heterosexuality*. New York: HarperCollins, 1994.

Ogden, Gina. *Women Who Love Sex: An Inquiry into the Expanding Spirit of Women's Erotic Experience*. Cambridge: Womanspirit Press, 1999.

Pertot, Sandra. *A Commonsense Guide to Sex*, rev. ed. Sydney: Harper-Collins, 1994.

"Postpartum Loss of Sexual Desire and Enjoyment," *Australian Journal of Psychology*, vol. 33, 1981.

"Preliminary Research on Plasma Oxytocin in Normal Cycling Women," *Psychiatry*, vol. 62, no. 2, Summer 1999.

Raynor, Clare. *About Sex*. London: Fontana, 1972.

Reichman, Judith. *I'm Not in the Mood*. New York: William Morrow, 1998.

Schnarch, David. *Passionate Marriage*. New York: W. W. Norton, 1997.

———. *Resurrecting Sex*. New York: HarperCollins, 2002.

"Sex in Australia: Sexual Difficulties in a Representative Sample of Adults," *Australian and New Zealand Journal of Public Health*, vol. 27, no. 2, April 2003.

"Sexual Dysfunction in the United States," *Journal of the American Medical Association*, vol. 281, February 10, 1999.

"Sexual Problems: A Study of the Prevalence and Need for Health Care in the General Population," *Family Practice*, vol. 15, 1998

Szuchman, Lenore, and Frank Muscarella, eds. *Psychological Perspectives on Human Sexuality*. New York: John Wiley, 2000.

"Third Annual Female Sexual Function Forum," *Medscape Women's Health*, vol. 5, no. 6, 2000. www.medscape.com/viewpublication/128_index.

Weiten, Wayne. *Themes and Variations*, 3rd ed. Pacific Grove, CA: Brooks/Cole, 1995.

Index

Underscored page references indicate boxed text.

Behavior
  biological influence on, 38–39
  sexual
    culture influencing, 54–55
    gender differences in (*see*
      Gender differences in sexual
      behavior)
    variations in, 27
  societal influence on, 32, 34, 36
Beliefs, sexual
  society's influence on, 36, 197–98
Biology, influencing gender
      differences in behavior, 38–39
Blame, avoiding, in sexual
      relationship, 163–64
Body image problems, 145–47
Body language signals, for ending
      foreplay, 187
Bondage/discipline/sadomasochism
      (BDSM), 110–11
Books on sexuality, sexual illusions
      created by, 14–15
Boredom during sex
  causing mind wandering, 149–51
  overcoming, 185–86
Brauer, Alan, 15
Brauer, Donna, 15
Breast stimulation
  as irritating, 46–47, 48, 175
  as men's view of affection, 46–47,
      170, 175
Brief sex, advantages of, 63–64, 187
Brothers, Joyce, 5
Burning vulva syndrome, painful
      intercourse from, 118–19

C
Casual sex, prevalence of, 52
Change
  in communication, 202–3
  encouraging woman's attempts at,
      178–81
  prerequisites for, 126, 128
  taking responsibility for, 209–11

Childbirth, low libido after, 97
Chronic conditions, sexual problems
      from, 115–17
Clitoral stimulation, orgasm from, 8,
      13–14
Clitoris, anatomy of, 40, 119
Comfort, Alex, 14–15
Communication
  I-language for, 159–60
  of man's emotional needs, 175
  negative
    affecting relationship, 114
    affecting sex life, 65, 202
    changing, 202–3
    origin of, 201
  nonverbal, role of culture in,
      54
  positive, for strengthening
      relationship, 114, 201–3
  problems, as factor in anti-libido
      cycle, 78–79
  about sexual needs, abandoning
      rules about, 64–65
Compulsions, sexual, 109–11
Conception, importance of orgasm
      to, 41, 49
Confidence, as essential to good
      communication, 78–79
Conflict-resolution strategies
      for arguments, 205–6
Conformity vs. individuality, society's
      value of, 21
Contraception, effect of
  on sexual pleasure, 7, 13
  on women's view of sex, 7–8
Counseling, when to seek, 161
Crenshaw, Theresa Larsen, 15
Criticism
  damaging effects of, 201
  as sign of relationship problems,
      146
Cultural values, influencing sexual
      behavior, 54–55
Cybersex, 110

Fatigue
  limiting orgasm, 143
  postnatal, low libido from, 97
  sexual avoidance from, 59
Female sexuality
  conservative 20th-century views of,
    4–6
  cultural shift in views on, 6–9, 13
  current expectations of, 3–4
  effect of contraception on, 7–8
  redefined by Masters and Johnson,
    13–14
Fetishes, 109–11, 172
Fisher, Helen, 39
Focus during sex
  for improving sex drive, 149–51
  for improving sexual relationship,
    155–56
Foreplay
  with breast and genital stimulation,
    46–47, 47–48, 175
  in non-demand sex, 186
  overemphasis on, 74, 187
  signal for end of, 187
Frequency of sex
  abandoning rules about, 63
  mismatched, creating concern
    about low libido, 73–74
  normal variations in, 25
  relationship problems as obstacle
    to, 46–47
  sex therapists' view of, 22
  sex therapy for increasing, 31
Freud, Sigmund, 4–5
Friendship
  of couples, as key to happiness, 200
  mutual respect in, 207–8

G

Games, sex, 61, 110–11
Gender differences in general behavior
  anatomical influences on, 42–43
  biological influence on, 38–39
  from social conditioning, 32, 34, 36

Gender differences in sexual behavior
  anatomical influences on, 42–43
  biological influence on, 38–39
  evolutionary theories about, 39
  male stereotype in, 33
  media influences on, 36–38
  media portrayal of, 34
  other influences on, 43–44
  physiological influences on, 39–44
  relationship behavior and, 44–46
  from social conditioning, 33, 34
  social conditioning influencing, 36
  summary of, 50–51
  usefulness of, for reaching sexual
    potential, 35
  as viewed by early sex therapy,
    32–33
Genital stimulation. See also Vaginal
    stimulation
  as irritating, 46–47, 48, 175
  as men's view of affection, 46–47,
    170, 175
Goal-oriented performance, Masters
    and Johnson's views on, 8
Goals, sexual, establishing, 30c31
Goodwill
  in emotional relationship, 208–9
  importance of, 183, 184, 206–9
  as relationship goal, 212
Gottman, John, 200, 205–6
Gray, John, 39
Gregersen, Edgar, 11
Guilt, from refusing sex, 77, 156–58
Gynecological problems, sexual
    problems from, 117–20

H

Happiness, from friendship of
    couples, 200
Hassle-free sex
  components of
    emotional triggers, 192
    environmental triggers, 193
    non-demand sex, 185–88

positive self-talk, 190–92
sensory triggers, 188–90
from relationship sex, 184–85
Health problems, as cause of sexual
problems, 115–20
Hilliard, Marion, 5
Hormones, role of, in sex drive,
40–41, 47, 48–49
Humor, in relationship sex, 60–61
Hygiene issues, as sexual turnoff,
93–94
Hysterectomy, loss of sexual pleasure
after, 119

I

Idealized beliefs about sex, 104–6
Ignorance, sexual
as cause of sexual problems, 84–89
in 20th century, 6–7
I-language
during arguments, 205–6
for communication, 159–60
Illusion, sexual, as created by mass
media, 15, <u>16</u>, 17–18
Importance of sex, variations in
ranking, 27
Individuality, sexual
lack of acceptance of, 28
variations in, 22–28
Individuality, society's value of, 21
Inhibited ejaculation, 44
causes of, 47
help for, 26
sexual problems from, 102
Initiation of sex
as factor in anti-libido cycle, 75–76
imbalance in, 26
by man
fear of rejection in, 166, 167
flexibility in, 168–70
by woman
difficulty with, 154–55, 166
male reactions to, 54–55
Insight therapy, drawbacks of, 209

Internet pornography, 110
Isolation, as factor in anti-libido
cycle, 82

J

Johnson, Virginia, 6. *See also* Masters
and Johnson

K

Kassorla, Irene, 15, 33
Kinsey, Alfred, 13
Knowledge, as essential to good
communication, 78

L

Laumann, Edward, 9, 10
Liberation, sexual, definition of, 22
Life events, as cause of sexual
problems, 94–99
Lifestyle
as cause of sexual problems, 90–94
as obstacle to emotional closeness,
203–5
Listening
in good communication, 79
to sexual needs, 65
Love
expression of, 54, 175–76
sex and, 44–45, 52–53, 54–55
Low libido
in men, 10, 23
in women
blamed on pathology, xi–xii
after childbirth, 97
core issues behind, 71–72
menopause and, 96
prevalence of, 9, 23
from psychological problems,
101–3
reasons for, as explored in this
book, 9–10
testosterone replacement
therapy for, 40, <u>131</u>
upbringing and, 33

Relationship sex
abandonment of rules in, 61,
63–68
benefits of, 59–60, 61, 156, 184–85
for couples with lifestyle problems,
91, 92–93
after difficult life events, 99
example of, 62
for hassle-free sex, 184–85
individualized for couples, 68–70
men's acceptance of, 167–68, 171
overview of, 58–61
purpose of, 58–59, 121
rejection of, for erotic sex, 143
Resentment
of refusal, in men, 176–78
during sex, analyzing feelings of,
132–33
Respect
in friendship, 207–8
importance of, 183, 184, 205, 206
in relationship with partner, 208,
212
Response, sexual
normal variations in, 25–26
stereotype of, 23
Response style, variations in, 26–27
Responsibility for change, for
strengthening emotional
relationship, 209–11
Rules about sex to abandon
on awkward or clumsy sex, 66–67
on communicating sexual needs,
64–65
on duration of sexual sessions,
63–64
on enjoyable sex, 68
on frequent and regular sex, 63
on refusing sex, 66–68

S

Schnarch, David, 15
Self-stimulation. *See*
Masturbation

Self-talk
negative, as problem, 191–92
positive, for increasing sexual
interest, 188–90
power of, 190–91
Sensory triggers, for increasing sexual
interest, 188–90
examples of, 189–90
Separation, as factor in anti-libido
cycle, 82–83
Sex addiction, 106–7
Sex drive. *See also* Sexual desire
female
anatomy and, 42, 43
biology and, 39
complexity of, 46
men's rethinking of, 163–64,
166–67
menstrual cycle and, 40–41, 47
mood and, 47–49
narrow definition of, 134
physiology influencing, 39–42
relationship satisfaction and, 45
variations in, 43–44
low (*see* Low libido)
male
anatomy and, 42–43
biology and, 39
consistency of, 44
evaluating, 164–66
physiology influencing, 39–42
unaffected by mood, 47
normal variations in, 25
viewed by early sex therapy, 8
Sex education
information excluded from, 86
lack of, in 20th century, 7
Sex games, 61, 110–11
Sex therapy
addressing traumatic past events
in, 102–3
classifying sexual problems in,
127
example of poor advice in, 16

gender differences viewed by, 32–33, 33–34
goals of, 31
Masters and Johnson's approach to, 8
methods in, for solving relationship and sexual problems, 53–54
for perfectly normal women, xii
reasons for seeking, xi, 198
relief provided by, 125
sexual abuse explored in, 101–2
sexual frequency viewed by, 22
sexual potential viewed by, 28
unrealistic expectations of, 125
Sexual abuse
confronting offender about, 101–2
sexual problems from, 28, 29, 99–102
Sexual behavior
culture influencing, 54–55
gender differences in (see Gender differences in sexual behavior)
"normal," stereotypes about, 18–19
variations in, 27
Sexual beliefs, society's influence on, 36, 197–98
Sexual compulsions, 109–11
Sexual dependency
characteristics of, 107–8
of men, 76–77
Sexual desire. See also Sex drive
emotional vs. physical, 25
expressing feelings of, 153–55
normal variations in, 25
polarization of, as factor in anti-libido cycle, 80–82
sexual response vs., 25–26, 142
subjective definition of, 23–24
unrealistic expectations of, creating concern about low libido, 73
Sexual fantasies
for improving sex drive, 147–49
for male sexual arousal, 43

about other men, 148
about rape, 149
unusual, 44
Sexual frequency. See Frequency of sex
Sexual goals, establishing, in relationships, 30–31
Sexual ignorance
as cause of sexual problems, 84–89
in 20th century, 6–7
Sexual illusion, created by mass media, 15, 16, 17–18
Sexual individuality
lack of acceptance of, 28
variations in, 22–25, 27–28
desire vs. response, 25–26
ease of arousal, 26
frequency of sexual activity, 25
importance of sex, 27
initiation vs. response, 26
robustness of desire, 25
time to orgasm, 26
type of desire, 25
variation in response style, 26–27
variety in sexual behaviors, 27
Sexuality, female
conservative 20th-century views of, 4–6
cultural shift in views on, 6–9, 13
current expectations of, 3–4
effect of contraception on, 7–8
redefined by Masters and Johnson, 13–14
Sexual liberation, definition of, 22
Sexual needs
communicating, 64–65
separating sexual wants from, 171–72
Sexual personalities, 30
Sexual pleasure
from avoiding goal-oriented performance, 8
effect of contraception on, 7, 13

RODALE

MACMILLAN